BURNING THE
WEALTH OF A NATION

Thank you
for buying this
book

21/10/23

BURNING THE WEALTH OF A NATION

The Nigeria Perspective

Michael Famokunwa

Published in the United Kingdom in 2023 by Framichi publications.

www.framichipublications.com

DEDICATION

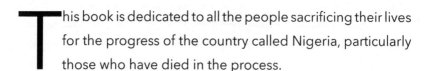

This book is dedicated to all the people sacrificing their lives for the progress of the country called Nigeria, particularly those who have died in the process.

ACKNOWLEDGEMENT

The author is grateful and indebted to all contributors to this book. The following are just a few from the long list of contributors: Johnson Akinwande, Titilola Soyinka, Folakemi Oluwasanmi, and Sylvia Olaiya.

I couldn't have written this book without the support of my loving family; my sons, Dele Famokunwa and Sope Famokunwa. Most importantly, the queen of the house, Dupe Famokunwa.

TABLE OF CONTENTS

LIST OF FIGURES AND TABLES

AUTHOR'S NOTE

◆•————————•————————•◆

This book aims to provoke a change in the approach to Nigeria's challenges, highlighting the untapped potential in the individuals and the nation. It can, in no way, be detailed enough because each topic touched is like a can of worms.

Wealth burning looks at how you as an individual manage available resources on the micro level and a nation's macro level. A review of the utilisation of resources at a scheduled milestone or a specified time reveals wealth created or burnt. Many situations lead to loss of wealth in the country, and little attention is paid to this due to poor management by individuals who then extend this to the organisations they work for.

A bad road not only causes delays to a journey but also increases fuel consumption compared to doing the same journey on a good road. It can also cause damage to the vehicle, which will take resources to rectify. Many roads around the country are in a state of disrepair because of bad management and poor maintenance. The same can be said of irregular electricity supply and availability of water for drinking and general use.

A nation develops when it addresses inefficiencies found in its system. A nation develops when there is continuity in government visions and accountability by the leadership. A nation develops when its citizens have something to share with other nations of the world and are proud of it.

Wealth is burnt when existing infrastructures are not maintained and are allowed to deteriorate to the point of abandonment. Wealth is burnt when infrastructures are not updated to the contemporary state as more resources are used to keep them going.

Remedial action can only be taken when how wealth is being burnt is recognised. Burning wealth is an ongoing practice; hence, a constant review is needed to minimise loss and continuous waste of resources.

Playing catch-up remains a bane and contentious issue for a developing nation like Nigeria. This is because efforts and resources are devoted to studying, understanding as well as maintaining what has already been done by the developed Nations. International standards are set in a way that developing nations are almost banned from the starting point of a contemporary issue. For example, Nigerian banks are not functioning properly, and the Central Bank of Nigeria is talking about a cashless society because the developed nations are moving towards it.

When emulating developed nations, Nigerian leaders should strive to provide essentials such as clean water for all its citizens.

CHAPTER

INTRODUCTION

Nigeria, for a long time, has been losing both human and natural resources. This is through extremely poor management. Efforts made to develop are defeated by unscrupulous and incompetent leadership. Therefore, many Nigerians spend a lot of time discussing various issues facing the country. It is evident that there are generations of Nigerians unaware of a time when clean tap water was in individual homes and that a rural electrification program was once implemented.

Today, electricity supply from the national grid only relieves the millions of generators used in many homes, offices, and industries. This alone has seen many companies collapse, with many leaving the shores of Nigeria. It also stops many international investors from citing their manufacturing plants in the country. It makes the development of local entrepreneurs difficult due to the extra costs required.

A program of operation 'feed the nation (OFN)' aimed at increasing locally produced food for the nation to be self-sufficient. As a result, River Basin Authorities were established in various states in the country. School children lived carefree and safely on the streets and in boarding schools.

The list goes on, and sadly, the country has been experiencing continuous degeneration, decapitalisation and falling standard of living for a while. These are in critical areas, so the positive developments in the country are eclipsed.

It is unclear if the leaders are unaware of these issues or why no fiscal measures have been put in place to turn round the ongoing degeneration experienced from year to year.

Nigerians have been able to put up strong resilience and ride out the challenges that rise with poor leadership. While many visions and ambitions have been killed, the spirit of many Nigerians remains high. While some have given up on Nigeria as one nation, others continue to strive for its survival.

Nigerians, have to their detriment, taken advantage of poor leadership, leading to a loss of probity across board. The onus has been on individuals to make the right choices; however, many do otherwise, knowing there will be no redress for their actions.

Based on the issues highlighted, the minimum expected from Nigerian leaders is the maintenance of existing infrastructure. Leaders should have this as a base for running the country, and the people should demand it. There should be a change in attitude from all.

It should be unacceptable to continually hear that Nigerian leaders are inept. The leaders must rise to the challenge of steering the nation in the right direction. This will mean the leaders setting out short to medium-term and long-term plans for the nation. The culture of each administration is deceiving the world by putting a hold on work/contract linked to its predecessor and then abandoning them should end.

Nigeria should not be importing basic petroleum products such as petrol or premium motor spirit, diesel, aviation fuel, or their derivatives. What plan has the Nigerian National Petroleum Corporation and the Minister of Resources in place to meet the increasing need of the growing population? The leaders must take responsibility for ensuring the availability of these products.

When will it become unacceptable to openly demand and give bribes? The situation where members of the public negotiate on how much to give police officers at check points should be unacceptable by Nigerian leaders and the people.

Police officers' training must be suitable and fit for the purpose. Hence, training facilities should be in place to achieve producing well-trained new recruits. Police officers should be well-paid and well-equipped to be able to police the country. The number of police officers should be increased. A police officer on the street should be in a standard and recognisable uniform. It should be mentioned again that the police force should provide the uniform its officers have to wear while on duty.

There are corrupt uniformed officers all over the world. But they do not operate openly and get severe punishments when caught. It is an open secret that senior officers encourage corruption. They expect and accept money made from corrupt officers (generally described as returns). Check points are set up simply to extort money from the public.

The police have become a threat to the public that they are meant to protect and serve.

There is a report by Sahara Reporters of a member of the public that was assaulted. The police did ask the victim to contact them. One would however expect the officer to report the incident in the first instance.

PR News has a report of the members of the public also assaulting police officers.

It is worth mentioning that many police officers have also been killed by criminals. Some are attributable to a lack of duty of care from their colleagues.

Planning for the future enhances continuity, accountability, and development. It is being done in progressive nations around the world. This is what the people of the nation should expect, and Nigerian leaders should take up the challenge.

Nigeria should be a tourist destination for people from all over the world as it is blessed with beautiful seas, beaches, and sunshine all year. The country has vast forests, mountains, and valleys for exploration. This is a challenge for Nigerian leaders; they should be selling the country to the world.

The streets of Nigeria will be kept clean if the government makes provision for that. In addition, they would be cleaner if everyone cultivated the attitude of not littering them.

Nigerian leaders and rich ones employ cleaners to keep their homes clean. They, however, do not think it is right to provide adequate facilities for the treatment of the garbage removed from their homes.

CHAPTER

BRAIN DRAIN

B rain draining from Nigeria remains the greatest wealth that its burning increases yearly. It was previously mainly among nurses and doctors but has now cut across all professions. Nigerian graduates cannot wait to emigrate, while those studying abroad do all they can to avoid returning to the country.

Every developed and developing nation puts in place a conducive environment to retain high skills. As a result, there is an international exchange of talents as people move from one country to another. Brain drain is, therefore, not peculiar to Nigeria. There is, however, the rise of a new paradigm known as the 'Japa generation,' people leaving en mass to anywhere but Nigeria. This is done without guarantee of a better life at the other end.

*Figure:2.1 Brain Drain (Source:https://mo.ibrahim.
foundation/search?query=brain+drain)*

The case with Nigeria is that disproportionally more talents are moving out. Nigeria continues to see locally-trained doctors, nurses, and engineers; its graduates from all faculties are leaving its shores. This is a serious double loss for the nation because the graduates and other professionals leaving the country have been trained at the expense of the nation.

News about Nigerians holding key positions in organisations and government departments all around the world where merit and hard work are recognised features regularly in the news. Nigerians abroad also excel in research leading to innovation in all fields across the globe.

There are many businesses owned by Nigerians in the diaspora. Fig 2.1 is a Nigerian baker who has branches in different parts of Canada, where he emigrated. These Nigerian entrepreneurs would gladly love to replicate their businesses in Nigeria if conditions were conducive.

Figure 2.2: Successful Nigerian in Diaspora. (Source:
*https://www.youtube.com/watch?v=cL_ADSaoIFc&ab_*
channel=NewsPopNG)

Talents are further lost when people with international experience return to Nigeria only to be frustrated and made to leave the country again. Some of these returnees lose their lives in their quest to give back to the nation.

There are incidents where returnees were kidnapped, tortured, and killed. Events like these stop not only nationals of the country but also foreigners from deciding to venture into Nigeria.

The following case is an extract from the social media on 05 August 2022; it is summarised on this Facebook link:

https://www.facebook.com/ArewaRepublican/posts/589173246187334/

It has been minimally edited to protect the family but not overly to ensure that their story is not distorted in any way. There has not been any contact with anyone in the family to seek permission to republish their experience. The information is readily available in the public domain.

"May God comfort the O family and friends on the murder of GO. GO was a hardworking perfect gentleman. He was comfortable in the United States of America (USA) but strongly believed in investing in Nigeria as part of his giving back by providing employment.

He has a farm in Ogbomoso, and he opened a hotel in the same town in December 2021. He was in Ogbomoso till March 2022. He returned to the USA and prepared for his final relocation to Nigeria in July 2022 after many decades of a successful life in the USA.

He returned to Nigeria few weeks ago and was kidnapped few days later. A ransom of five million Naira was paid. Yet the kidnappers killed him with two others.

Of the two others killed was a University Student who took up a job at the Hotel while waiting for inept ASUU and Nigerian government to resolve their problems. And she died making herself useful as a worker in a new hotel. GO also died while creating value to the society.

If he had known that his death would come this way, he would have stayed where he was in America. If he had known that

Nigerian Government has become totally useless, and that there is a limit to what an individual can provide for their own security, he would have stayed in his Maryland home in the USA. He owned a company in the USA.

Earlier today, I spoke with his elder brother - JOJJ , to condole with him, and we spoke extensively. JO was my former landlord, through whom I knew GO.

When we cry, we still see. It is obvious that the following set of people have contributed to the degenerated situation in Nigeria.

(1) The Obas - some of whom only survive in this chaotic government. Indeed, it was said that some Obas also share in the ransom payments.

(2) The Local Government Chairmen - most of whom don't even know their functions. They see themselves as more responsible to the State Governor than their local people.

(3) The State Legislators - many of whom lack reasoning and ability to make a meaningful impact. Many love pleasure than work.

(4) The Governors - they formed Amotekun to pay lip service to fighting insecurity. They do not equip them adequately. No training in an intelligent gathering. Kidnappers have better weapons than Amotekun. Yet these Governors take billions of Naira in Security Votes. The Nigerian Governors are the major enemies of the Nigerian people.

They are part of the inept National Council of State. They mostly determine who gets what at Local, State, and Federal levels. The Nigerian Governors are the most inefficient arm of government in Nigeria.

(5) The Nigerian people at large - they are not ready for real change. Many love to suffer and to smile. Many are not interested in the common interest of the society but in their personal interests. The people are not ready to say enough is enough to continuous decaying of the society.

I deliberately left out the Federal Government because that category is a perpetual failure. I even heard that some Nigerian soldiers share in kidnapping ransom. Only those listed above can bring real changes. There is nothing like Federal Government. It should only exist on agreement with those 5 categories.

CONSEQUENCES

(1) GO's death will affect the lives of many families who earn their living from his businesses in Ogbomoso.

(2) GO's death will heighten the fear and apprehension Nigerians in the Diaspora have for themselves and their family members. The decision to invest in Nigeria, let alone relocate there, will be far from coming."

The above case says a lot about the need for all Nigerians to take steps to reverse the degeneration of societal values at all levels.

The whole nation must address the rampant increase in kidnapping, ransom demand, and payment. Kidnapping has taken a new dimension in the country and continues to evolve.

This crime is associated with countries described as "failed" or "failing." Nigeria has failed to fight corruption, provide a safe society, or provide good health services. It is failing in its ability to use the available natural resources to improve the wellbeing of its citizens. Nigeria is failing to foster unity amongst its different ethnic groups.

The hard solution to discouraging or ending this atrocity is for the nation to agree not to pay ransom to fellow Nigerians to release their brothers and sisters. The situation will turn for good once the kidnappers do not expect ransom payments. Nigerians must rise to the challenge of not condoling this ill-means of extortion from fellow citizens.

The people of Nigeria must be empowered with knowledge, skills, and means to prevent kidnapping. All safe efforts must be made by potential victims to prevent the kidnap from taking place in the first place. This is so as the victim becomes powerless once in the hands of the abductors.

The confidence and audacity with which the abductors conduct their act can be undermined when they know that people will resist their wicked act. This can be taken further if the whole society looks after each other. The extreme will be for more Nigerians to carry arms in self-defence.

It must be made clear to society that the abductors are a minority in the country. Hence, they can be defeated by the unified will of the majority. The scary atmosphere created should be defused and the associated fear removed.

Each citizen of the country should be able to exercise the right to live freely in any part of the country. No one individual's life is more important than the other, thus demanding equal protection.

The continuous and quick payment of ransom demands has put total control in the hands of the abductors. They have used their barbaric treatment of their victims to achieve this. Society can take back control by collectively agreeing that ransom payment is no longer the norm.

The government must lead the "no ransom payment" campaign and educate the nation accordingly. The security agencies must not be found wanting in the crusade to seek and bring the abductors to justice. No abductor should be at peace as often said, "No peace for the wicked."

The government should bust the hideouts of the terrorists cum kidnappers. The Nigerian forests should be taken over by state governments to develop into game reserves for safari-style tourists experience where possible.

Those who publicly act as intermediaries for ransom demands should be arraigned before the courts and not be allowed to earn a commission for their evil acts. It is absurd that notable Nigerians can be seen to be colluding with those who terrorise the citizens.

The citizens' role is to be the eye for the safety of their societies and say no to what they do not want. They are to provide a welcoming and safe environment so that their communities would be places where people enjoy living. This will encourage immigration rather than emigration.

Many graduates from the many Nigerian institutions should end up living and working in communities close to their institutions of study or where they carried out their National Service. International students should also want their visas extended after their studies to remain in Nigeria.

Many have gone to establish today's leading corporations providing contemporary products and services. The same can happen in Nigeria if measures are put in place to stop the brain drain and encourage the immigration of international talent.

This is to stop the brain drain and provide locally sought-after skills. The result will be a cosmopolitan society with people working collaboratively and moving the societies forward.

LEADERSHIP

The need for the best leader should be the desire of every nation. A process should be in place that allows the selection of the best leadership candidates.

No one person should be superior to another citizen of the nation. As a result, everyone should be ready to work under the elected leadership. The notion and demand that one religion is superior to others should be debunked at the highest level.

Various well-documented leadership styles are available to apply in running an organisation. It is essential to have strong leadership in place to ensure that the goals and objectives set are steadfastly pursued. While achieving the objectives remains the goal, visible leadership actions drive the vision.

Nigeria has been failed by the leaders it has had in the last forty years, for none of them can claim to leave a tangible achievement as a legacy of their tenure. A developing nation like Nigeria has so many areas that a leader can focus on to take the nation to the next level in its development. It is disheartening that businesses cannot function properly today. In fact, many are folding up simply because of interrupted power supply.

It is equally disheartening that water supply to each home is still a long way for many homes in Nigeria. The health implication should have been a good driving force for a leader to want to pursue having a national grid for sewage. Unfortunately, this is not the case; each house is also left to sort its human waste. It is not surprising that water borne diseases prevail in the country.

Why do students and lecturers at the nation's universities still go on long-time strikes yearly, resulting in courses taking much longer than planned?

Table 2.1: ASUU Strikes Over the Years
(Source.www.eduplana.com)

Year	Duration (days)
2022	242
2020	270
2018	90
2017	30
2013	150
2011	59
2010	150
2009	120
2008	7
2007	90
2006	3
2005	14
2003	180
2002	14
2001	90
1999	150

Strike actions by recognised bodies are healthy for expressing dissatisfaction against issues that need resolution. However, strikes over the same issue by the same body as the ASUU year after year are a display of failure. This is so because the issues leading to the strikes remain almost the same. Agreements reached were either short-termism, issues not fully resolved, or adequate measures not put in place to prevent future strikes.

Nigerian leaders do need to raise their game so that the same mistake is not repeated. Nothing is indeed new under the sun; there is a solution to every social issue confronting the people of Nigeria.

In some cases, it is simply wanting to improve the current situation rather than allow stagnation or deterioration. This is why it is ridiculous and wicked of the leaders who continue to leave the shores of Nigeria for medical treatment abroad. It is callous of them not to be encouraged to want to improve things at home by what they saw abroad in medical facilities and the service they received.

It is also unclear why history is allowed to repeat itself. The status quo remains in an evolving world. For example, the Independent National Electoral Commission (INEC) makes people register for elections and request that the voter visit an office to collect their registration card. It becomes a situation where millions of people visit an office when INEC should deliver the cards to voters with their registered addresses. It will need thousands of people delivering to millions of homes rather than the former.

Figure 2.3: Chaos at a voter card collection office
(Source: Sylvia Olaiya)

The delivery of voting cards by INEC will save many mishaps when people travel from afar to collect voting cards. It saves individuals time and money because they can go about their normal duties. They will not need to take time off work or pay transportation costs to INEC's designated offices. No stress or frustration resulting from queues at INEC's offices for the voters and equally for INEC's frontline staff who have to deal with the frustrated public.

*Figure 2.4: Patient Nigerians waiting at a voter card
collection office (Source: Sylvia Olaiya)*

INEC leadership and competence should be at stake as Nigerians are made to suffer so many inconveniences to collect their voting cards. There is no accountability to anyone, and therefore, no questions asked or answered.

It has been put forward that the decision to make each voter collect their voting card is to ensure it gets to the registered voter and avoid malpractices. The counter-argument is for INEC to work with credible partners and put a process in place that each card is traceable to ensure safe delivery.

The work involved in getting Nigerians to have a voice to vote in elections should not be restricted to election times only. INEC should be working all year round not only to ensure its register of voters is

21

up to date but also to reach more of all eligible voters and increase the percentage of eligible voters that are indeed registered.

Figure 2.5: Election day, voting in progress
(Source: Nike Fadairo)

No movement was declared on election day in Nigeria, no trading, no work, just go out and vote and go back to your home. Credit should be given to the government, INEC, and every Nigerian who saw that the election went as scheduled. It is a welcomed development for the country.

Issues relating to safety, physical fighting, and killings during electioneering campaigns would be refined over time as Nigerians adopt and refine the act of democracy. Our politicians will learn not to openly offer money for votes. People will know there is no reason to kill fellow citizens because of a transient political office or on behalf of a politician. People will know that all politicians attend the same social functions and are professional allies.

There are situations where husbands and wives belong to different parties, one in the ruling party and the other in the opposition party. They scream and challenge each other in heated political matters and events. They arrive and leave in the same vehicle. This is a good reason for all to passionately engage in civil and peaceful elections.

Figure 2.6: Election Day, Feb 2023
(Source: Sylvia Olaiya)

Figure 2.6 is a typical polling station on the election day conducted on 25 February 2023. There is room for improvement from INEC on the state of polling stations like the one shown above. Voters in many stations had to wait for the arrival of the polling staff. This is not acceptable. Punctuality is very important; it allows for proper planning of the diary. The polling staff should be ready and waiting for voters by the publicised opening time.

A good analysis shows a few lapses. What will happen to the documents on the table should it start to rain or there is a gust of wind? For example, security, health and safety risks in the immediate surroundings are of concern.

The February 2023 elections highlighted other issues, including Nigerians' mixed attitudes in different parts of Nigeria. Some were violent, while it was people enjoying what they had been given by the political parties. Many Nigerians queued to cast their votes, as in the figure below. It is hoped that the positives of the 2023 elections will be an encouragement for many more Nigerians to vote in future elections.

*Figure 2.7: Voters Queueing to Vote During the February
2023 Election (Source: Sylvia Olaiya)*

They are expected in an election everywhere in the world. They are lessons that enable the country to better prepare and conduct future elections.

It is hoped that Nigerians will refine their attitude and approach to elections with every election. Nigerians should work towards having fun and enjoying elections by watching the politicians battling. This was what the people in Lagos Victoria Garden City did; they had a barbeque while voting.

Nigerians must take on board that open and wilful destruction of ballot materials was not done by INEC officials, nor did they carry out violent acts during the elections. Nigerians will collectively stand against those who chose violence during elections. It is a form of robbery that should face severe punishment in a society where law and order prevail.

Figure 2.8: Relaxed Victoria Garden City Voters
(Source: Sahara Reporters)

Nigerians should pay attention to how they approach those they vote into office. They are to be respected and assisted in doing their public service. The act of seeking favours leading to everyone servicing the politicians should be reversed.

The act of seeking favours from people in office may have led to a group of governors' wives being accused of going to Dubai to celebrate the birthday of the wife of the then-president. The wives came out to refute the allegation stating they were in Dubai for a different assignment.

The president's wife would have done better if the day had been spent at an orphanage in Nigeria or at an event organised for the less privileged in the country. The governors' wives, on the other hand, could consider similar events in their individual state to celebrate the occasion.

The opposition parties and politicians really do not play their role well in taking the government to task. While it can be argued that everyone has a right to choose where to live or spend more of their time, the mother of the nation should live amongst her people. She must be seen actively doing things in the country while occupying the position of authority, whether budgeted for or not by the nation.

A good opposition should have no problem demonstrating that the wife of the Nigerian president should be resident in the country. There are lots of ways the wife of the president of a nation can motivate the citizens of their nation. This should not

be done from abroad and/or across the ocean.

The above narrative shows Nigerian leaders' lack of vision and/or misplaced priorities.

A key area that a leader can focus on to deliver what benefits the people is to provide a good road network for the safe transportation of people, goods, and services. So many roads in Nigeria can be made a joy to use only if they are tarred properly.

The leaders have been able to get away with a disservice to the people because of the lack of a unified voice from the different corners of the nation. Imagine if the whole country agrees that quality education funded by the government for everyone up to a certain age is made compulsory.

The absence of a unified voice has consolidated power in the president, who continues to take advantage of the situation. The president has become unaccountable to anyone, and no one dares to question his inappropriate actions or decisions.

There is a need to carry out the devolution of some of the powers of the federal government through legislation to enable state governments to carry out some of the functions they are currently excluded from is under active consideration.

The state governors, too, must review prevailing legislation to see powers that can be devolved to local governments who are the ears of the electorate. This will enhance local development in the first instance and the nation as a whole. The leaders and the man on the street will work together as the people's voices are heard from the local government to the federal government level.

Imagine if the whole nation demanded from its leaders in one voice that university lecturers should not be allowed to go on strike for more than two consecutive weeks and not more than four weeks in an academic year. This means any dispute must be resolved within a very short period. A process can be put in place that allows an adjudicator to make a pronouncement that is bidding on both parties.

It is said that the result of a task is very dependent on the leader. The leader who appoints on merit does get projects delivered. A president that fails to recognise the disadvantages of appointing heads of establishments in Nigeria from a section of the country is bound to fail in many things. The failure will be compounded by the fact that the international world will also be aware of the incompetence of the appointees.

The post holder is undermined as their appointment was not on merit. Table 2 below gives the holders of key positions at a time under a government.

POSITION	POST HOLDER
Minister of Defence	Bashir Magashi
Minister of Police Affairs	Maigari Dingyadi
National Security Adviser	Babagana Monguno
Inspector General of Police	Usman Alkali Baba
Chief of Army Staff	Faruq Yahaya
Chief of Naval Staff	Awwal Gambo
Director General of SSS	Yusuf Bichi
Director General of NIA	Ahmed Rufai
CG of Customs	Hameed Ali
CG of Immigration	Isah Iris Jere
CG of Prisons	Halliru Nababa

CG of NSCDC	Ahmed Abubakar Audi
Chairman of NDLEA	Bubo Manwa
CG of Federal Fire Service	Abdulganiyu Jaji
Corps Marshal of FRSC	Dauda Biu

Table 2.1: Holders of Key Positions in the Nigerian Government in 2019 - 2023 regime.

The names of the holders of those key positions in Table 2.1 would mean nothing to an open-minded researcher who believes in rewarding skills and competence. The thought would have been that they have been appointed with the interest of the nation as a primary objective. The view will likely change when a fair understanding of the crave for and control of power in Nigeria are considered.

In a well-publicised long-awaited interview, the president openly said on air at prime time that he appoints only those known to him. He unknowingly affirmed that his appointments were and will not be based on merit. Therefore, the appointees have nothing to prove in office, so there goes probity, responsibility, and accountability.

The Nigerian constitution makes provisions for its government to reflect the federal character. Successful organisations strive to have a staff composition that reflects their society. It pulls talents from all competent people, so every customer is at ease with the organisation due to the diversity of its workforce.

Appointing loyalists rather than competence means performance is never measured. Therefore, the issue of poor performance, mismanagement, or inefficiency is thrown out of the equation. There is no target set to measure performance and no benchmarking with successful bodies around the world. This is why Nigerian officials do not resign when their positions become untenable for whatever reason. You never hear of the sacking of an obviously failing and underperforming post holder. Many officials do not appreciate what it means to become unfit for their positions; no shame or integrity is at stake. There is the failure of the appointing president to reprimand his known appointee. The president rendered an intelligent vice-president useless and unproductive for whatever reasons only the president can reveal.

'Nigerianism' is killed and not taken into consideration as the appointees equally think and act like the president that appointed them. They, too, appoint those that they know, and that trickles down the ladder. Everyone in a position of authority is "oga's pikin" (oga means boss, and pikin is literally child but could be mole, spy, loyalist, etc.). You cannot touch *oga's pikins* whether they are right, wrong, incompetent, fraudulent, looting, mismanaging, wicked, unfair, or destructive. This is a concoction for lawlessness.

The selective appointments were reflected across all national bodies. The myopic vision led to inefficiencies, corruption at all levels, and deterioration of all services as standards are compromised daily. Nobody can hold anyone accountable in any government body as the head of each body was basically powerless. Powerless simply because they were not appointed on merit. No one has been dismissed from office for being inefficient, considering the visible deterioration of services and infrastructures in the country.

The president at the time deprived himself of talents from other parts of the nation, thus causing more dissent and division amongst the people of Nigeria. Pursuing selection by merit will result in a solid government that delivers in all areas of society. The approach should simply be to give the remit of needs to be done and then find who best can do it rather than slotting less competent people.

Suppose the case is that the appointments were on merit. In that case, the systems and academic institutions that produced such a cohort should be reviewed. How is it possible that successful candidates only come from a section of the country?. Not only people known by the president should be appointed to key positions, but also competent people who can be trusted to get the job done.

A good leader will gain the trust of those in key positions, and they, in turn, will trust the leader. Seeking security and loyalty by appointing mediocre is a fatal step to take by any leader. It cripples each organisational body that it is practiced.

Unsurprisingly, the result of that government was a total breakdown of law and order. The country experienced increased terrorist attacks on people and property, with military establishments not excluded. Schools had to close because of fear of an attack and the kidnapping of students and their tutors.

Progressive organisations seek diversity in their management; they pool the best talents, enabling them to deal with contemporary issues in the best way. They all have long-term resilient plans in place for the future stability of their institutions. They plan not only for future progress and development but also disaster prevention and recovery from one.

This cannot be said of any head of a Nigerian Government establishment. None has come up with a medium to long-term plan for their establishment. Below is the experience of an industrialist whose national interest was killed by the personal interest of a Nigerian in a key position. It is sourced from www. nairaland.com, and the content captures an attitude that needs to be turned around in the interest of the nation. It is hoped that on reading it, many Nigerians in places of decision-making will henceforth look beyond their personal interests.

"As I look at the recently concluded world cup series, I am saddened by the performance of the Green Eagles.

While many people know of my foray into software development for the country, I seldom talk about other projects I attempted to execute in the country as part of my contribution as a Diasporan who wanted to give back.

A friend in this group called me today to ask and wonder why the 360 degree turn in my attitude towards the country and why I am so embittered. I laughed and said nothing. After careful deliberation, I thought it was time to share more of my experiences while I sojourn in Nigeria.

Criticism of Diaspora is completely misplaced.

People need to understand the quiet pain and losses we endure for our country.

Once I settled down in 2016 and felt (a false) a sense of security about my investments in Nigeria and the critical development work I was doing for the country, I considered another undertaking.

I was angered by the massive number of Nigerians watching the European Soccer league. I imagined the economic benefits to Europe and financial losses in foreign revenue, lost jobs to Nigeria

I approached the minister of sport in 2017 through a mutual friend and assured him we could bring soccer to international standards in Nigeria. We could set a healthy minimum salary (in millions), create over 100,000 direct middle class jobs in the first year, and over 250,000 indirect middle class and low income jobs.

The minister was dismissive at first. He had been approached with similar offers that never materialized, and I understood his scepticism.

I assured him that I don't start anything if I can't finish it. I am a pitbull of sort when I embark on a project.

I assured him I would bring $1 billion dollars to the game in Nigeria. He practically laughed me out of his office. So, I issued him a challenge.

If I could bring the money to the table, would the ministry grant me a license to start a new league in Nigeria.

He looked me up and down as if to size my capacity to deliver, then chose to take me up on my challenge. Personally, nothing excited me more than a healthy dose of challenge.

I immediately returned to the US. Put a team together. A friend who had played with Atlanta Falcons and ran a semi-pro football team in Atlanta introduced me to a number of sport agents, which led to an introduction to a major sports management group based in NY. I quickly engaged the group to put a league and marketing plan together, a $75k project. My team in Atlanta put the business plan together, and within 30 days, we were armed with a pitch document. I went into sport equity market pitched several equity firms, leveraging my businesses, and i successfully secured a $750m letter of credit (LOC) with terms to draw subject to the issuance of license promised by the minister.

I returned to Abuja and the minister was presented with LOC, I have never seen a black man turned white before, as he could not believe I had an LOC for $750m. I assured him we would supplement the funding with a licensing fee to be issued to 10 club owners at $25ml each, which would complete the $1bl guaranteed to the minister.

The league will fund $50ml to each team, creating a $75ml escrowed capital to launch each club.

Leaving us with $250ml to develop the league

We began to test the market for broadcast licensing agreements to fund our LOC payback. Interest was strong and the numbers made sense.

There are more people watching soccer games in Nigeria on a Saturday than the UK, Germany, and France combined. The export market for Nigerian soccer league games across the globe is mature. There would be little or no distance between us and Brazil if we did things right.

Nigeria was licensing Euro soccer games and exporting foreign exchange and to me reversing that trend was a personal objective.

We submitted our business and marketing plan to the minister, including economic impact. He was excited and all on board. The secretary to the Ministry of Sport was on vacation while all these were going on. The legal department engaged us, and an agreement to issue a license was put in place. Negotiation ensued and terms agreed upon. "It's execution time" just needed the secretary to return from vacation.

USL (United Soccer League) was about to be a reality.

We would take over existing federal and state stadiums for 10 clubs and bring them up to international standards with corporate suites.

We were going to leverage the first year of broadcast license to attract retired BIG name international stars like Ronaldinho, Kaka for 1 yr contract or borrow some international star to help launch the league. The clubs making up the league would have to bid to join our first year.

We set our season opposite European league to give us room to grow with minimal competition for our audience.

This was an exciting development for me as things moved along.

Secretary to the ministry returned, and our discussion on agreement was now at his desk, expecting things to move forward. Then came the jolt from all directions.

Suddenly, there was talk about buying the existing NFL, something I vehemently opposed. You can't take a bad product and wrap it in a new package and expect the audience to buy it. There is a reason the NFL is not captivating the attention of Nigerians, but we can help it develop, not acquire it.

Also, we feared we would run into conflict with existing, compromised structure under the control of entrenched personalities.

We offered to put $50ml into the NFL to improve it and allow it to feed players into the USL (United Soccer League) which would increase the value of the NFL and we would share stadium with them to improve value of their broadcast license fees.

Not only would we have triggered massive, minor-league development across the country, we would have develop local stars to international status, with similar benefits as enjoyed abroad, retirement programs, health coverage, multi million naira contracts, super star statuses.

I remember introduction to the great Kanu by an assistant to VP Osinbajo and a few other greats in the football space in Nigeria. The excitement was definitely brewing.

I had people working on both sides of the Atlantic working on league rules, marketing, retail licensing, security, trademarks, and other intellectual rights.

Then, the bomb shell. The secretary of the ministry decided to send the agreement to outside parties for review.

It was the last I ever saw the agreement. The agreement left the building and never came back. Inquiries after inquiries yielded nothing.

I was disillusioned, I had put my credibility on the line for the LOC. I had triggered costly activities at numerous organizations locally in Nigeria and in the US.

Suddenly, I got a call from an unknown number. It was a male voice on the other line.

Who is this I asked?

Response : Oga it's not important, I just want to tell you that things will go well if you can at least leave 5% of this project for the people at the ministry.

I was stunned left speechless for about 60 seconds.

5% of $750ml is $37.5ml where on earth do you hide that on your books and how do you allocate and describe that expense to your investors.

That was the end of my soccer project in Nigeria. I promised I would not participate in corruption in Nigeria and stood by it.

2 years later, I completed my primary and robust project for Nigeria. Tested and approved to launch in 2019. 45 days before the launch date, a demand came forward that could have easily put me on the radar with the US government and in violation of the US foreign corrupt practices act. I declined.

2 weeks before we were to launch the project for Nigeria, I was verbally advised that the head honcho has decided to stop the project. He was no longer interested. It was no longer about Nigerians. It was about his personal interest and decision.

The cost to me personally was significant financially, with several million dollars just discarded by head honcho of the government agency. I also lost a network of investors and sustained damaged credibility with one of the largest sports equity funds in the US

I left Nigeria and promised only to return for family matters only.

Nigeria died inside me.

To all those who want to criticize Diaspora, please understand that many of us tried and, in many ways, failed. You, the people, just don't know or hear about the sacrifices we make. It's a horror show.

We love our country as much as you do. When you say we are online and just posting and agitating, there are reasons for it.

Nigeria is a crime scene, a burial ground for our investments, life savings, and retirement."

Questions:

1. What makes a good leader?

2. As the new president, head of state, and commander in chief of Nigeria, what will be a priority project, and how should it be implemented?

3. What is national interest?

4. Appointment by merit can lead to development. Discuss?

5. Should there be a difference in National Interest and Presidential agenda?

6. Why should the National interest be the Presidential agenda?

CASE STUDY 1: In the academic year 1986/87, the government closed the universities for five consecutive months. The lecturers were on full pay while the students were at home. Some students never returned to complete their studies. The then Head of State found it convenient and okay to delay the development of its youth. What could have taken five months to resolve? Discuss.

CASE STUDY 2: In June 2019, students at an institution of higher learning went on the streets following the death of a fellow student due to poor health facilities on site. There was no ambulance to transport the student to a nearby hospital. What are the failures in this scenario?

HUMAN RESOURCES

Nigeria is endowed with a vast amount of human resources; it has a population of nearly 200 million people. The unfortunate truth is that very little value is placed on life in the country. There is still a very poor process for recording births and deaths in the country.

Unproven news abounds that people and body parts are being used for rituals to make money. Lives are being destroyed daily by heartless gangsters, cultists, and spiritualists. Unsurprisingly, people disappear without a trace, and bodies are found in open spaces regularly all over the country.

Nigerians today kill themselves over a variety of reasons ranging from religious, ethnicity, political rivalry, and greed to just wickedness. Those deemed to be making progress become targets in their communities and are eventually killed. This attitude is so ridiculous that an achiever available to help others is taken out. Their visions are killed, as well as those of the people that depend on them. This self-damaging practice should be reviewed and put to an end.

Nigeria has not invested adequately in the education of its people. A visit to some primary and secondary will highlight the state of the education system. Well-equipped science or music laboratories are hard to come by. Teachers are hard to find in the classrooms as the majority no longer rely on their salaries but spend valuable teaching time pursuing other businesses to guarantee food on the table.

Nigerians do not focus on solving a problem but take a backward remedy or focus on just the way to make money. The culture of research and development is not prevalent in the country. The result is that human potentials and associated skills are not adequately explored.

Brain drain is not limited to Nigeria, as earlier stated. Nations all over the world develop themselves to become attractive to people in what is termed economic migration. The recruiters specialise in talent hunts around the world to get the right person for the requirement of their clients.

The person head-hunted from another country becomes an emigrant with everything in place. There is a job to go to and the right to stay and work in the country they are going to. They plan their journey and travel safely to their destinations.

The other group of emigrants goes through underground

methods, including using people traffickers to just get to another country, mainly in Europe. They arrive at a port they most likely have not heard about before. Some take a popular treacherous journey crossing the Mediterranean Sea from North Africa to Europe.

Figure 2.9: Wreckage of Migrants Ship
(Source: BBC News Feb 2023)

At least seventy-two people lost their lives in the mishap of just one of those boats across the sea. Figure 2.9 shows the remnants of the boat used to ship people into Europe. People pay to travel through Libya or another North African country to cross over to Europe. Countless lives have been lost on this method. Many do not even leave the North African country as they are made to work in a way equivalent to that of an enslaved person. Sadly, some do die while doing the hard, laborious work.

Those who succeed in getting to Europe become refugees in the new land. The beginning of another journey to regularise their staying and living in this new place. Their first solid soil in Europe may not even be the country they are migrating to. How long it takes to get there is a question that can be answered by those who have made it this way. It is different for each person.

The ideal route is the traditional way of getting a visa to enter another country for a purpose. Life is ever-changing. Suppose you need to extend your visa for a different reason. In that case, Living a restricted life as an over-stayer in another country is still possible.

This is how the issue of living illegally in another country arises. Your visa runs out, and you fail to return to your country. You become part of the black economy and exploited by those specialising in taking advantage of people in such situations. This may continue for years, and while this is the case, you cannot travel to another country or seek the right employment. You are restricted in the jobs you can do and have no voice.

Many Nigerians have also fallen as victims of scammers who promise so much to prospective emigrants. Some give up all they have in Nigeria and sell assets, including houses, to pay intermediaries who promise to get them abroad. They give up what they have for uncertainties and, for some, total disappointment.

It is best to seek advice and assess all options when considering migrating to another country.

QUESTION:

What is dangerous about crossing the Mediterranean Sea to another country without a valid entry document?

CHAPTER

ACCOUNTABILITY
AND RESPONSIBILITY

Accountability is simply taking responsibility for the role given to someone. A line is drawn to highlight the limit of the remit of a particular role. This is to allow collective decision-making in an organisation.

Under no circumstances should an officer be able to usurp the power of other role(s) within an organisation without colluding with other people.

The budget holder should be clearly known, visible and linked to the position. That person must be ready to deal with any underperformance and address inefficiencies in their department.

Regular updates should be provided to assure all that the post holder is aware of the position of things within the department and is actively involved to see that expectations are met. The updates promote transparency for people and encourage wider interests and contributions. This is because critics from a wide audience will give comments and advises.

A culture of continuity will be developed, enshrining ownership and commitment.

Position of authority has been abused in many cases in Nigeria; Organisations, including banks, have collapsed due to misuse of the power that goes with key positions.

The budget set and agreed upon is to ensure the smooth running of an establishment. A budget is monitored regularly to highlight the position at set times for corrective action to be taken. An example is a board of governors for a primary school that set up an account dedicated solely to salaries. It is therefore not surprising that staff are paid timely and regularly as expected.

In Nigeria, it is not unusual to hear that staff have not been paid for one or two months or that pensions have not been paid for even longer periods. These two simple examples show failed accountability. Pension providers and employers would know when an employer is due to retire well before hand. They should liaise with each other and the employee to confirm when the first payment will be expected. There should be no break moving from being paid a salary to pension payment. It should be a seamless transition.

The consequence of non-regular payment of salary/pension leads to stagnation in the flow of goods and services. This is so because there is a break in the cycle of economic activities. The unpaid worker cannot pay house rent, meaning the landlord becomes unable to make their financial commitment.

The unpaid worker will also be unable to buy food from the marketplace. Then the seller too becomes unable to sell their goods and services. This then leads to delays in placing orders from the manufacturer/supplier.

The farmer may be unable to sell the perishable items, which will lead to a loss of produce, thus making the farmer poorer.

The scenario above highlights that everyone is very important in the supply of goods and services.

The irregularly paid worker then needs to find an alternative source of income to replace the unpaid salary. This will include loans from sources such as banks in the form of overdrafts, friends to family members and buying goods/services on short-term credit.

The fact remains that the unpaid worker must find money one way or the other, which has led to the development of the culture of not relying on a monthly salary. This is probably why the culture of bribery and corruption has become part of most establishments, though unacceptable and a norm in society.

QUESTION:

What are the implications of untimely repayment of loans and total default?

CASE STUDY: The term for the Director of Works of a tertiary institution, a Nigerian University, was coming to an end. The outgoing Director conducted a recruitment process, ensuring the preferred candidate succeeded.

The result was cancelled by the ruling council following reports that the answers to some questions by some of the candidates had been tampered with. Another recruitment process was conducted, and the candidate initially deemed the best came out trumps again.

The result came out through the grapevine, and the highly anticipated news swiftly went round the department, but only for a while. The result was not officially announced. Why? Again, another malpractice took place.

Questions:

1. Why does the outgoing director want a particular candidate to take over the role?

2. How can the institution restore confidence in its recruitment process?

3. What should be done to the outgoing Director?

CASE STUDY: A University lecturer was found guilty of misdemeanour and dismissed from his role. His offence was he had a relationship with his female student for marks in his course. This is not new, but things went badly wrong when the story went viral on social media. He has brought shame to the institution and undermined the hard work of so many other lecturers and students.

Discuss the case with recommendations on how to ensure it does not happen again.

REFLECTIONS: The above two case studies are events that occurred in two leading universities in Nigeria. These are institutions meant to produce future leaders for the country. Their failure to have in place a system that prevents high-level corruption reflects the situation in many other institutions, organisations and the country in general.

The culture of having one person in total control of an organisation without check should be frowned upon in all institutions. Banks have been brought down by reckless/corrupt chief executives who dipped into the assets without security. It explains why banks collapse because of internal abuse.

BUDGETING

A budget is simply a schedule of income and expenditure to ensure that a project goes to plan financially and timely. Similarly, it ensures that a department is run smoothly. A simple example is budgeted salary for an organisation over a fixed period. A budget should be reviewed as often as reasonable or prescribed within the period to ensure things are going as budgeted. This will enable corrective measures to be taken to bring it on course. A staff salary account or any account with funds restricted for staff salary ensures that salary is paid as promised by the organisation and as expected by the employer.

It is clear from above that it is necessary to have the resources to make a budget succeed. It is, therefore, unwise to proceed with a project without making provisions for the necessary resources. Consider a state government that has no money to make regular salary payments to the whole of its workforce, who suddenly had a windfall, then decides to start paying monthly pensions to people of pensionable age. Do you think this is sustainable on a long-term basis?

It will be useful to find out how many payments each pensioner received and why consequent governors abandoned the gesture. It was not a thought-through policy that was budgeted for. It was probably just a scheme to treat some funds as spent on pension payments.

National and federal legislative policies should exist for issues like pensions and bursaries for higher education students. The federal government sets a standard amount from its budget, and individual states can then have their additions to it.

There is a need to have both short-term and long-term plans. A strategic plan with clearly defined goals must be in place. A five-year plan is ideal for a nation like Nigeria.

Budgeting financially quantifies a plan. It can be for a small or big project broken into minute tasks. Planning ensures the feasibility of a project because provision is made for the financing of every stage. A government that can successfully present a budget will carry its people along the journey in the financial year. The people will be able to accommodate the necessary adjustments made due to prevailing circumstances that are well communicated.

CHAPTER

LIVING STANDARD

The picture below shows about eight naira exchanged for one American dollar in November 1990. Just over three hundred and fifty Naira is needed to get one dollar as of June 2019. The value of the Naira to the Dollar can be compared to what it was in 1990, whenever this book is being used. It will reveal which way the country's monetary policy (if any) is heading.

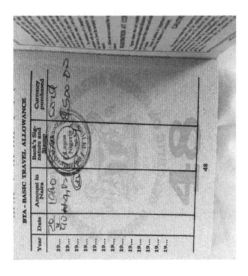

Figure 4.1: Basic Travel Allowance (1990)

The naira has depreciated significantly against the dollar. This is a depreciation of nearly 4500% over nineteen years. The public may not experience such a high depreciation of the money in their pocket. Those importing goods and services will feel the impact seriously. Nigerians studying abroad requiring regular remittance from home too will feel the impact of the fall in the value of the naira.

The biggest contributing factor to the fall in the naira's value is that Nigeria is a net consumer of imported goods and services. Nigeria has petroleum but still imports petroleum products such as aviation fuel, petrol, diesel, colas, and the list goes. Nigeria has not mitigated the continuous fall in the naira value by increasing its exported goods and services, increasing proportionately locally produced consumables, or changing its culture of preference for imported goods over locally made ones.

It is worthy of highlighting the impact of money being stolen from the country by people in places of trust. People with access to the money that should be used to construct necessary infrastructure for economic development.

The amount being taken out by individuals has increased over the years, and so too, is the number of those carrying out the practice. Another practice that has gained ground is keeping stolen money anywhere but in the bank. Properties are rented in Nigeria to store money; soakaways are also used with water tanks becoming money tanks as money is stored in them.

Figure 4.2: Example of money found in storage
(source: Sky News, Pic: EFCC)

People carrying out the practice of storing money out of the banking system are not sympathetic to the needs of the nation.

The proper use of banks to keep money support productive ventures which create employment, thereby eradicating poverty. This also would help slow down the rate of depreciation in the value of the Naira.

Money kept out of the banking system may be lost in full should there be a policy change by the government. One of such policies was redesigning the naira notes announced late in 2022.

The old naira notes in Figure 4.3 are being hurriedly retrieved from the many out of banking systems where they have been stored to be circulated into the economy. This was attempting to beat the initial deadline of 31 January 2023 set that will make old notes unacceptable as legal tender. This shows shortcomings on the part of the owners of money kept out of the banking system.

Figure 4.3: The Nigerian Naira (Source: Voice of Nigeria)

Case study: Discuss the impact of increased rice or maize production on the Nigerian economy.

Case study: How can each state in the country support its local manufacturers?

Case study: How can the general populace be convinced to prefer locally made produce?

Case study: Why do people store a lot of money outside the banking system, and what will you do with an appreciable amount of money.

STANDARDISATION AND QUALITY
OF GOODS AND SERVICES

The efforts of different bodies trying to ensure Nigerians get good quality products and services must be recognised and commended. Little progress has been made as some staff connive with stakeholders that should have been prosecuted or made to improve the quality of their services.

The issuance of a warranty is a guarantee of the quality of a product or service. It makes parties in a contract responsible because expectations are set, understood, and agreed upon.

A good service provider would have a procedure for addressing customers' complaints and dissatisfaction. They compensate their customers for any shortcomings resulting from not meeting customers' expectations. The complaints and losses incurred to redress their shortcomings enable them to improve and innovate.

The government officials from statutory bodies intervening in some cases promote the culture of who is known or how much can be paid to get out of the hands of the law. Many cases have been swept under the carpet because of this.

Figure 4.4: Road Revitalisation Project May 2019
(Source: Femi Awolusi)

Figure 4.4 above shows the static position of a revitalised road in Nigeria. Looking at the equipment on site for a project of this magnitude indicates the standard and quality of work that can be done. It shows efforts being put into the guttering. The road itself is likely to be levelled without any solid ground reinforcement. It will then be coated with asphalt to give a glossy finish, a finish that will not stand following torrential rainfall or the passage of heavy goods vehicles.

The status quo has been maintained; the guttering will soon be filled with rubbish, sand and, of course, stagnant water. These are all health hazards that the road design should have considered at the conception stage.

Figure 4:5 The Standard finished Road in Nigeria
(Source: Pic by Femi Awolusi)

This is a typical example of a substandard construction project. It will not be farfetched to conclude that what was delivered was not what was paid for. Repeat this all over Nigeria to

have an idea of how much is lost by the country through substandard projects. The impact on development and sufferings this practice brings on the Nation is massive.

The question remains why Nigerian professionals are comfortable delivering substandard goods and services to their own people. The question should also be asked of those responsible for ensuring that goods and services are of a minimum standard. The contractor and client have both studied very well to gain professional qualifications but failed to apply the acquired knowledge meant to enhance real development. It appears that no pride is taken for good quality and long-lasting legacy. It is terrible for the nation that people are not responsible for delivering poor-quality goods and services.

There is a need to change the mindset of the people. Nigerians must want to deliver products of good quality. Every Nigerian is responsible for the required change, not just the government or private sector. This is the way to stop resource waste through poor-quality goods and services. Equally, Nigerians, too, must demand high-quality products and services.

PROFESSIONAL BODIES

Professional bodies such as the Institute of Chartered Accountants of Nigeria (ICAN) exist in societies to regulate and ensure high standards of goods and services. They give credence to their certified members; a reason people aspire to register with the relevant bodies related to their trades. They also give confidence to members of the public because their members are expected to be qualified and experienced in their fields. Therefore, the work they do should be of high quality and come with a guarantee.

Figure 4.6: The Nigerian Academy of Engineering
(source: Michael Arpil 2023)

It is puzzling why many members of these bodies offer substandard service with little or no reprimand.

Where are the auditors when there is continuous embezzlement in public corporations in Nigeria? The auditors have become part of the corrupt system in their ability not to uncover malpractices. Listed below are some well-known bodies in Nigeria that should put the country on par with similar bodies in developed nations.

1. Institute of Chartered Accountants of Nigeria

2. Nigeria Society of Engineers

3. Council for the Regulation of Engineers in Nigeria

4. Nigeria Bar Association

A good reputation is a marker for professional bodies and their members. This is achieved by providing highly quality standard products and services.

A professional organisation holding a position can severely damage its reputation when its members provide poor service or product. Every effort should be made to ensure that quality is not compromised.

This gives rise to a knowledgeable market of buyers and sellers of services. There is healthy competition amongst all.

Quality is comprised in most cases because of the funds available for the work. The process of securing a project such as road rehabilitation, for example, entails money changing hands at various stages. The situation is exacerbated when there is a need for a bank loan. There is bribery in the process.

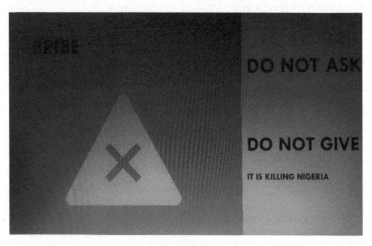

Figure 4.7: Bribe, killing the Nigerian economy.

In some cases, contracts are awarded based on connections rather than competence. This is common in different spheres of the Nigerian economy. The big breweries allocate products to distributors only on paper, which, in turn, sell the allocation to traders down the line. It is practiced in the cement industry as well to cite two examples.

The result of the malpractice is inflamed market prices for consumers. While the citizens can decide on which product to buy, they have no such choice in capital projects. The money has been siphoned along the line, leaving little or nothing for the work.

The padding of the national budget is a known and accepted practice in Nigeria. This a poor example of probity by the legislators who should lead in the battle against corruption. Little or nothing is heard from them in terms of improving the process to make people shun corruption.

It is worthwhile to highlight the role some countries take to help fight corruption. They have laws against bribery; one of such laws is that their companies must not offer or take bribes.

Case study: Do Nigerians know they should demand good quality goods and services? Discuss why and how it should be done.

Case study: What are the obstacles to providing quality goods and services in Nigeria?

CULTURE

The love of money, they say, is the root of bad things. This simply means that people do anything to get money. People behave like a bulldozer let loose and brings everything in it as it goes through a forest. The field will the littered with fallen trees, some fully rooted out of the ground, some partially and occasionally, some will be left unscathed. In some cases, there is regret due to unintended damage.

There is a need to define what is expected of people in a society so that everyone clearly understands such. A nation is unique only in its name. This is so because all nations have their own share of the good, the bad and the ugly practices. Each good, bad or ugly practice becomes relative based on a particular nation's tolerance level and focus.

While culture and tradition are interwoven, a society must be ready to modify medieval traditions that should no longer be tolerated. Rituals for different outcomes are on the increase in Nigeria. The rituals require parts from specific animals and defined parts to similar specification from human beings.

The above practice is one of the reasons some people disappear in Nigeria and are never found. The fact remains that some people in Nigeria do this as the service they provide and derive their living from it. They request their clients to bring specified animals or parts thereof and similar requests for fellow human beings. Do they tell the clients where to get the human body parts or make them lose their senses to reduce a human being to raw material for their desired product?

How do you explain a house help employed to assist with chores in the house deciding to poison their employer? The loss of care and compassion for humanity is absurd. There is no better way to highlight this than the case of a seventy-two-old woman who was a victim of this barbaric act. View this on the web:

https://onlinenigeria.com/stories/314135-man-arrested-for-cutting-off-nipples-of-72-year-old-woman-for-money-ritual-in-anambra.html

A search on the web will reveal many such unpleasant incidents like the one above.

There are cases of shop assistants selling stocks belonging to them in the shops they are employed to manage. This act does not take into account the overheads borne by the employers. This means that the shop owner must be at the shop whenever it is opened to minimise losses from its own paid staff.

The wicked, selfish, self-interest attitude of the Nigerian people must change. Nigerians must take on board the attitude to do what is best at all levels for their employers. There is the driver draining fuel from the fuel tank or swapping good tyres for bad ones. The driver buying fake vehicle parts instead of the original ones paid for. These are actions that will later impact the resources of the driver's employer. There is the possibility of running short of fuel in a remote area, structural damage from tyre blowout to loss of life.

The fact is that many Nigerians at all levels either do not understand or do not care about the consequences of their actions. It is solely because of not seeing the overall picture and forgetting the interlinking of their individual actions. Immediate self-interest tends to overrule, thus leading to a society of anything goes.

There is total mistrust at all levels of the Nigerian society. No one is trustworthy of being entrusted to carry out a transaction in a prudent way. Nigerians at all levels will break the vicious cycle of selfish interest. There is nothing bad in looking after one's interests. The fact that it is done to the detriment of others almost always makes it terrible for society.

Where has the saying *"Do unto others as you would want done to you"* gone? Do people just say it without understanding its benefits? You want the best for yourself, so you should also want the best for others. This leads to a win-win in all situations. *Figure 5.1* below depicts a house owner in Norway who has had a bountiful apple harvest. She bagged and hung out the fruits for members of the public to freely take away.

Figure 5.1: Freebie Apples in Norway
(Source: Drammens Didende)

This is looking after your neighbour while ensuring that good fruits are not wasted. Can you imagine Nigerians doing the same during the harvest season when many farm produce and fruits go to waste in the country? This would be caring for your neighbour rather than thinking of money all the time. The apple owner could have arranged for a buyer of the fruits but chose to be generous to other people.

Stealing is taking something that does not belong to one without permission and knowledge of the owner. It can therefore go undiscovered for a long time. Robbers, however, do the same but with violence. These are two uglies of any society. Thieves and robbers are wicked in their acts. As a result, neither of them has peace. This is because, as the saying goes, "There is no peace for the wicked." Nigeria is massively burdened by both, another reason for disinvestment in the country.

Resources earmarked for infrastructures such as roads, hospitals, electricity, and steel plant are lost through stealing and robbery. Nigerians should work towards creating a society where there is no need to commit either by working in the interest of their society all the time.

There was a Nebraska farmer who grew award-winning corn. Every year, he won the award for the best corn grown. One year, a newspaper reporter interviewed him and learned something interesting about how he grew it. The reporter discovered that the farmer shared his corn seed with his neighbours. "How can you afford to share your best seed corn with your neighbours when they enter their corn in the same competition as yours each year?" the reporter asked.

"Why, sir?" said the farmer. "Didn't you know? The wind picks up pollen from the ripening corn and swirls it from field to field. If my neighbours grow inferior corn, cross-pollination will steadily degrade the quality of my corn. If I am to grow good corn, I must help my neighbours grow good corn."

There is no better way than the understanding and wisdom of the Nebraska farmer to explain why Nigerians should be caring towards one another. No need to be selfish; share knowledge and skills so all can benefit. Knowledge sharing is easily found on the internet. It is to the benefit of anyone anywhere in the world.

Just as every customer wants a bargain purchase, so does the seller want to maximise a sale. A landlord wants to rent the property, and a tenant wants a place to rent to live. Why do people curse each other in the process of their negotiations? People should learn to always remain civil and polite. The seller only has to reject any derogatory offer from a buyer, hoping that a better will come. The customer is always right.

Saying yes and please with a smile go a long way in all areas of life. They are particularly very important for those who offer services to other people. A smiling shop assistant will draw more customers than those who look dejected or give the impression they would rather be elsewhere. That smile will also give rise to repeat patronage, hence, the shop's growth, just like the bankers providing good trusting services.

Nigerians should realise that society will be much better for everyone if due consideration is given to every individual action. *Figure 5.2* is a tweet from **@gimbakakanda** that summarises how Nigerians treat each other.

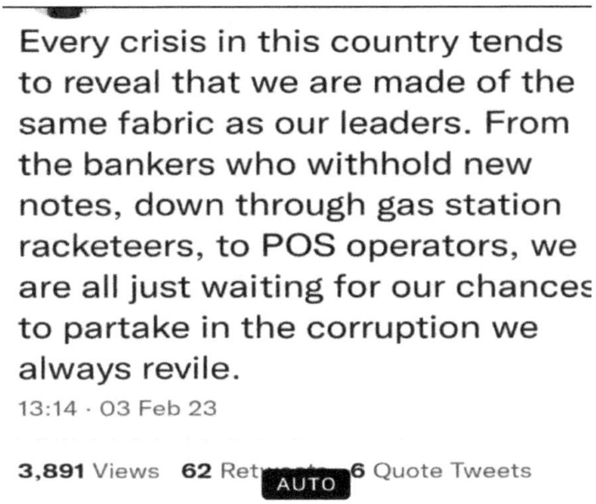

Every crisis in this country tends to reveal that we are made of the same fabric as our leaders. From the bankers who withhold new notes, down through gas station racketeers, to POS operators, we are all just waiting for our chances to partake in the corruption we always revile.

13:14 · 03 Feb 23

3,891 Views **62** Ret AUTO **6** Quote Tweets

Figure 5.2: Nigerians extorting Nigerians
(Source: @gimbakakanda)

Crises occur in every society in the world. It is not peculiar to only Nigeria. Every society deals with its crisis in different ways according to their culture. The best way to manage a crisis is to avoid it in the first instance. This is achieved by expecting a form of crisis and putting a plan in place for different outcomes, so there is no element of surprise. In simple terms, a detailed risk assessment and management are required. It should be mentioned that some natural disasters like earthquakes, flooding, and bushfires should also be expected and locally planned for.

Everyone is made aware of what to expect and advised what to do in very simple terms. Everyone means everyone, from the president to the person on the street. It must be highlighted here that crisis does not discriminate, not selective or biased in any way. People, however, put things in place to push the crisis away from them as much as possible. The result is that while they think they have relieved themselves of the crisis, they create more difficulties for a few but are indirectly affected as well.

When a crisis occurs, the plan that was made should kick in immediately. Organisations such as the Red Cross all step out to bring relief to those affected by a crisis. They put their Disaster Recovery Action Plan into play. The role of Victims Support is mentioned later in the book. Everyone should work compassionately to end a crisis to minimise its adverse impact on lives.

People do not live or work in isolation. Teamwork is the key to success, as each member's role is acknowledged. There is a collective responsibility. Project work in teams or groups should continue to be well encouraged because it leads to the development of soft skills needed in all areas of society.

After the crisis has been dealt with, a review is required to update the avoidance action plans and deal with future ones. The lesson learnt is so important and must be well publicised as they empower people to be able to appreciate their individual roles and importance.

Nigerian leaders, to date, appear not to have done the very least, creating awareness and preparing the public for any crisis. An avoidable crisis is allowed to happen time and time again in

Nigeria. This has led to a culture in the country where everyone, rather than working to ease the crisis, selfishly exploits it.

Figure 5.3: NNPCL Filling Station, Asese
(Source: Nairaland)

During the fuel shortages and old notes versus new notes prior to the elections in February 2023, the staff at the above NNPCL filling station did the greatest disservice to Nigerians. The station advertised a pump price of one hundred and eighty-nine naira per litre of petrol and allegedly surcharged one thousand two hundred naira per vehicle. That is taking over six litres of petrol from each customer.

They imposed additional conditions of no payment by Point-of-Sale facility (POS) but only cash payment using only the new notes. Chaos broke out when a driver refused to pay the one thousand two hundred naira levied. He was supported by other drivers. The station staff locked the pumps, stopped serving the people, and entered the office.

They were callous in leaving people to suffer. The fuel was available, and the people had their money. But a wicked and greedy set of fellow Nigerians refused to sell the needed petrol.

This was at an NNPCL petrol station; this is akin to running to who has the resources and what is needed to help when needed and being refused the help. It cannot be explained that an NNPCL station will refuse to sell petroleum products to Nigerians. It clearly reflects how NNPCL is run, with no care for the people of Nigeria. It is unable to refine petroleum to provide petrol for Nigerians. In this case, NNPCL refuses to sell petrol that is highly subsidised by the government to Nigerians.

How can the culture of extortion be stopped? The love of money builds the urge to take advantage of a crisis, thus making life more unbearable for others. It comes from the short-term view of the prevailing issue. The greed for money has overruled the urge to help to relieve another person from suffering.

Why is a bank withholding money from its customers? Nothing more than wickedness compounded by greed. A total failure of its function is to make money easily available to its customers when they need it.

The banks must remember that they are providing a service, and the interest of their customers should always come first. They are not doing their customers any favour by making their hard-earned money available on demand. Customers should not be begging for money or suffering to get it.

The banks should now invest in training their staff to have the right framework of what good customer service should be and how to provide it. Making more money for the bank will be achieved with good and trusted customer service.

Nigerians should develop and improve current customer care practices and provide after care services for their products. Customers pay for services and materials needed to rectify any defect in a product. Customers should not be requested or expected to provide the materials. Customers should be able to entrust their machine for service/repair to a provider and pay for labour and materials when the job is completed.

An honest shopkeeper will see the shop grow and make more profit, enabling the owner to give a salary increase voluntarily or when asked. It will create a warm environment for all, customers, workers, and owners. The employer will want the employee to work for them for as long as they want because trust has been established.

Lack of trust is a stress factor that seriously affects people in Nigeria. Very little attention is paid to it. Many people have died because of the constant stress they went through. Some of these deaths, without medical evidence, have been blamed on other people only to cause relationship problems and further mistrust.

Thus, the required change starts with each Nigerian deciding to do things with careful thoughts of the implications for other members of the society. This should be in all areas of life. A good and simple example is being honest as well as reliable.

Questions:

1. What is good customer service?

2. At what point should a customer be told off for crossing the line while negotiating a purchase?

3. Why is the customer always right?

4. How can one become trustworthy?

5. List five cultural practices associated with Nigerians that have grown well and are of good benefit to Nigerian society.

6. With relevant examples, state the implications of being nice to people without expecting a reward.

7. Why will one always benefit from being fair and upright?

6

POWER AND POLITICS

There is the belief that the interest of the nation is usually not the driving force of who turns out to be the president of Nigeria. People are not appointed to key positions on merit. It is made worse by the key personnel being surrounded by poor-performing loyalists.

The blatant abuse of the power bestowed by the office is unfair to society and inadvertently to the favoured, who becomes a liability for all. The favoured find themselves in positions they have no drive or visions for. They do themselves an injustice by taking up posts they know are beyond their capabilities, either by experience, knowledge, or skills. These people act like robots because they always say yes to the demands of their aforementioned *ogas*.

The states in Nigeria are suffering at the highest level based on the practice of restricting positions to indigenes of the state when more qualified and competent people are available from other states and even internationally. There is a loss of innovation and development. Key decisions are made based on sentiments, affiliation and pressure rather than on what is best for the State.

The nation suffers tremendously from a lack of continuity in policies and development. There is an uncountable number of revoked and abandoned contracts at both national and state levels. The norm is for the incoming government to start everything from scratch, not considering the financial cost of such an action. The Ajaokuta Steel project is a prime example of how different governments have failed the nation by not taking it to completion. While this practice is not peculiar to Nigeria, other countries do not make it a norm to abandon major projects that enhance development.

Nigerian politicians are well paid, but sadly, they do not acknowledge the need to deliver basic needs for the people. They do not do any benchmark with counterparts in the world.

Not too long ago, a politician took his four wives to the house to show that he was a strong man. He went on to tell the house he had twenty-seven children and still counting at the time (Nairaland).

Surprisingly, this lawmaker was not only given the audience to elaborate on how strong he is but was also cheered on by other members. Unfortunately, he was not questioned about what facilities he had established in the communities where his children would live. Neither was he asked of the other social-economic issues associated with a growing community. A reasonable and considerate leader plans and puts basic needs in place to accommodate population increase.

How he can combine his work with fathering so many children is beyond understanding. There are four full-time housewives, houses to maintain, and domestic waste and sewage to deal with. It will be interesting to know how these daily needs are met by the constituent of the lawmaker in question.

While one side will argue that the lawmaker is free to have as many children as he desires, this will be acceptable in a society where basic facilities such as water, road, medical care, schools, roads, etc., are in place. It will be excused if the masses are not suffering due to the misappropriation of public wealth by the so-called lawmakers.

Civilised societies make adequate provisions for growth in their population by birth and net migration. It should be hard for a citizen to justify having twenty-seven children. A lawmaker has, however, openly led the way, highlighting this as a feat showing he is a strong man. Others may therefore want to do the same. Nigerians must, however, make it clear that having so many children who will be brought up in a society that lacks basic amenities like water and healthcare is not a responsible act.

Questions:

1. What is not good about having twenty-seven children?

2. What should the other members of the house have done?

3. Will a man with twenty-seven be able to do his job properly? Discuss.

4. What training should be given to people like the lawmaker with twenty-seven children and still counting?

5. How much will it cost to raise twenty-seven children?

6. What is the Ajaokuta Steel Project all about?

7. Why is the Ajaokuta Steel Plant not completed after over forty years of signing the contract?

8. Discuss the lost opportunities because of the management

of the Ajaokuta Steel Project with reasonable financial estimates.

9. Starting with local consumption of steel and steel products, why have consecutive Nigerian governments failed to bring the plant to life?

10. What products from the Ajaokuta Steel Plant can Nigeria export, and discuss its impact on the country's foreign exchange?

JUDICIAL SYSTEM

The judicial system is one recognised big problem facing the country, but little is said about it. Justice is rarely delivered in high-profile cases, in fact, at all levels. This is so because of interference in almost all cases going through the courts. Judicial injustice allows corruption to be the order of the day. Every criminal, including politicians alike, knows there will be no punishment for their criminal acts or, at worst, will get a minimal custodian sentence.

Further mockery of the judicial system is that its pronouncements are very skewed. A section of society does not get a prison sentence but is given house arrest for the same crimes that others get incarcerated for.

This is impunity from the top and abuse of power.

There is no fear of justice being served by fraudsters and corrupt public servants; they get away with their loot and enjoy the proceeds of their crimes. It is on record that those found guilty under one government are pardoned when another government gets into power. It is also on record that Nigerians convicted of crimes in other countries return to Nigeria only to be celebrated and worshipped. There is a breakdown in law and order at all societal levels.

There is a need to create a condition and atmosphere of trust in the nation's judiciary where the people can rely on its judicial system to uphold the law and deliver fair justice in all cases.

At the other end is instant justice merited to petty criminals by members of the public. These are criminals caught while committing the crime or attempting to escape. The people around at the time descend on the culprits, hitting them with whatever is available. In some sad cases, they set people alight and burned them to death. This has continued in Nigeria due to a total breakdown of law and order and a lack of trust in the police to act with probity.

Case Study: Select a person that was imprisoned abroad. On release and return to Nigeria was celebrated as well as become a power broker. Discuss how the international world will perceive this.

SECURITY AGENCIES AND ARMED FORCES

It is public knowledge that the Nigeria Police is overstretched in terms of officers per thousand of the population. They are not paid well nor well-equipped. Police officers have fallen as victims at the hand of armed robbers and kidnappers. It is terrible to say that police officers also fall victim to men in the Nigerian Army.

They have been abused physically and fatally for issues as little as traffic incidents. A police officer in uniform should not be attacked by any military officer. There should be a process in place to deal with any matter causing conflict between members of the Nigerian armed forces.

The lawless state of Nigeria allows this to happen, as no one is accountable to anyone. Appointed heads of services who do not merit the positions bestowed upon them cannot call anyone to order or reprimand.

Any incident resulting in the death of a police officer is expected to be investigated until the perpetrators are brought to justice. This is not the case in Nigeria; armed robbers kill police officers. The cases are forgotten after a few weeks, not even a year. This is not surprising because some police officers aid some of the men of the underworld. This is a disservice to the fallen ones and a discouragement to potential officers.

Law enforcement bodies in the country should be working in unity and collaborating with their international counterparts. This will enable reliable and trusting processing of information at all levels.

LAWLESSNESS

It is often said that where there is no law, there is no offence. Nigeria has become a state where laws are ineffective and do not serve the purposes they were meant for. Nigerian leaders have made a mockery of the nation's laws in different ways.

Past and present leaders have failed to ensure that the nation's laws are properly implemented. Some have acted beyond the laws and remained in office. A past leader annulled a general election because the candidate preferred by some country elites did not win. This is impunity and total disregard for the law and interest of the nation.

The situation at play is anyone can get away with any crime in Nigeria. Your freedom is in having and being able to reach the right contact person before mob justice is enforced. Mob justice is prevalent in Nigeria due to the failure of the state to provide justice in the country.

The ease at which criminals are let off in the courts has empowered them, thus letting them continue their criminal activities. It has also led to a continued increase in the number of criminals at all levels in the country. They operate at will, knowing the public is defenceless. Equally, the public breaks laws at will, knowing that law enforcers are never around to enforce the laws. The thoughtless way Nigerians drive on the roads is worrying. It leads to stress, accidents, and chaos. *Figure 6.1* was taken as a passenger through the windscreen of a moving car.

Figure 6.1: Chaos on the Road, Ibadan April 2023

The vehicles on the left are in their legal lanes. In contrast, the car in the centre and others to the right took over the lanes meant for vehicles going in the opposite direction. What makes situations like this uncontrollable is that leaders in convoys with sirens, rather than staying in their lane, do exactly the same.

The leaders treat lawlessness with a carefree approach as they fail to stamp down on those who break the laws. This is simply because those in a position to enforce the laws are lawbreakers. A president that cannot provide a traceable declared academic history says it all when the integrity issue is raised.

Equally, a leader that campaigned to stamp down on foreign medical treatment only to make routine foreign medical trips after being voted into office. Here is a clear demonstration of a lack of integrity and an affront to the electorate. There is a failure from the top should the case be that other people are being curtailed from going on foreign medical trips.

Lawlessness brews a loss of compassion. This has become evident in Nigeria. People kill fellow citizens with no remorse or fear of retribution, as nothing is expected in the way of punishment. The Nigerian leadership does not even care to make it a duty to record each life lost resulting from the lawlessness that has gripped the nation.

It will be useful if each state is made to record and document each birth and death from the national figure would be obtained. The trend can make clearer the negative impact of lawlessness in the country.

Lawlessness creeps from the society's approach to governance; it is either "rule of law" or "rule by law". Nigerian leaders have not made their choice clear, as it is neither the latter nor the former. This is a reason for the chaotic lawlessness in the country. If some citizens are above a nation's law, the rule of law cannot prevail. Similarly, where some citizens are assured of protection from law enforcement agencies, then rule by law fails.

International agencies work together to bring to justice suspects and known criminals. Extradition is very difficult when an offence is deemed to have been committed in the course of duty on behalf of a state. This leads to a sour relationship between concerned nations. The opposite is when extradition is successfully carried out. It is known that some relations just refuse to cooperate in executing some extradition requests. Some Nigerians have taken solace in their country after falling foul of the law in another country.

Future leaders should aim to reverse the increasing trend of lawlessness, a number of criminals and criminal activities.

THE BANE OF NIGERIA

BASIC INFRASTRUCTURE

A good network of roads which connects all communities is needed for safe, cost-effective movement of people, goods and services. The rail network is ideal for bulk land transportation and mass movement of people. There is a lot of room to develop these transport media in Nigeria.

Telecommunication facilities must be upgraded and made available to parts of the country. The internet has enabled virtual working. It is now possible to do some jobs in any part of the country and the world.

Electricity is the power to drive every industry and domestic machine. The government should seek and form alliances with global players in electric generators. Nigerian leaders have no shame. If they do, action should have been taken to see that electricity is made available to all parts of the country.

There is no set target in place aiming to provide electricity to a certain percentage of the population by a certain year. No goal, so there is nothing to strive for. No measure of performance in place and no consequence for failing to improve what is inherited from the previous administration.

Wanton destruction of infrastructure should be avoided as it is a double loss for the public. Lack of contemporary basic infrastructure is evident in the Country, and for the people to destroy the little and archaic available facilities is uncalled for.

A peaceful demonstration is a simple way of getting a message to the relevant authorities as well as informing the whole world about a particular issue. Demonstrations should be well organised by recognised organisations responsible for directing those who support their causes.

Looting of shops, and burning properties, including public buses/coaches, are examples of what should not be done to existing infrastructures. It should be highlighted that some infrastructures, once destroyed, will never be rebuilt. At the same time, in other cases, lasting financial ruin may befall business owners. It is much easier to destroy than to build. A destroyed service provider may never provide that service again.

The cost of clearing the aftermath of a burnt building can be used to provide other services. This initial funding may have to be sourced in a frantic way as it was never budgeted for, and, in an ideal situation, it can come from an emergency fund if such a provision is in place. In most cases, funds will be diverted from other commitments.

Reconstruction costs could be overwhelming that the destroyed infrastructure is not replaced. A decision may be made to just make the site safe and make the people suffer for their actions. A change in decision maker may put redevelopment on hold. This is not progressive; however, this happens if existing infrastructure is rendered unusable.

The number of Police stations and public buildings that have been burnt by causes other than accidental fires is of concern. Nigerians must stop this act.

The consequence is the loss suffered by all. Firstly, as beneficiaries of lost service and secondly, as the provider of the services, thus leading to a poorer society. History is eroded in some cases, with no continuity and lost specialties. Also, it is a discouragement to potential local and international investors. No one would want to invest in a society where their assets could be destroyed.

THE BANE OF NIGERIA

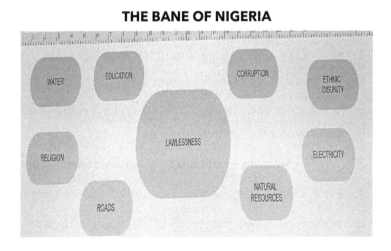

Figure 7.1: Barriers to Nigerian Development

Electricity

The amount of money spent daily to run generators for domestic consumption is difficult to quantify because there is no electricity from the national grid. It is even more complex, considering that most of the fuel is imported. The conclusion is that the country consumes much more than it should if the homes have an adequate electricity supply.

The nation's foreign reserve is being burnt because of this. This contributes to the depreciation in the value of the Naira.

Running a generator to produce electricity does have hazards such as fire, electrocution, smoke poisoning and security. Starting with the last, armed robbers sometimes target properties running an electricity generator. There have been many fire incidents relating to generators and, in some cases, loss of lives.

QUESTIONS:

1. How does running a generator in the home cause a fall in the value of the Naira?

2. What risks and dangers are associated with running a generator, small or big?

3. Why is electricity important in Nigeria's development?

4. How is Nigerian's wealth burnt through lack of electricity?

5. How will improve the supply of electricity in Nigeria?

6. Identify how electricity generated is wasted or used illegally and how to remedy this?

LAND TRANSPORTATION ROADS

A good network of roads connecting all communities, including farms, is key to the safe movement of people, goods, and services. This is, however, where a great disservice has been dished to Nigerians. The roads where they exist are not motorable, deplorable, or encourage daylight robbery by the local self-appointed team raising charging users for maintenance work.

A road that is properly constructed should be able to give at least twenty years of good motoring. There will, of course, be wear and tear as well as natural disasters that can adversely reduce the life of a road.

Figure 7.2: Section of Third Mainland Bridge, Lagos
(The Eagle Online)

As mentioned earlier, Nigerians continued to be short-changed because many roads were poorly constructed. They are not solid enough for heavy goods vehicles that end up using them. No guttering is provided to address drainage, nor is proper signage for all users.

RAIL NETWORK

Figure 7.3: Nigeria Rail Corporation (Source: nrc.gov.ng)

The Nigeria Railway Corporation (NRC) has been in existence for over 112 years. On its website, it described Nigeria as a geographical area. Progress is being made in this area. Each state should consider linking its towns by rail by working with the NRC. The goal is a rail link from state to state in Nigeria and then to neighbouring countries like Cameroon in the east, Niger in the north (this has been done) and Togo to the west.

Figure 7.4: Modern Train in Transit (Source: nrc.gov.ng)

Rail transportation is vital for the safe mass transit of people and goods. It creates ongoing employment for people in a variety of industries.

WATER AND WATERWAYS

Nigeria has ample water resources to tap for the use and development of its people. There is a lot of room to use waterways for moving people and goods from one place to another.

There are more than enough seacoast lines for local and international tourism. There is a need for more port terminals in the country.

There is an unacceptable shortfall in the supply of drinkable water in homes in the country. Individuals are left to invest heavily in different ways to have water to use. This has led to scrupulous suppliers of poor-quality water who get their water from different sources, including rivers.

No government, either at the state or national level, has improved the water supply into Nigeria's homes since the 1980s. What is happening is a continuous loss of supply into homes. This is the opposite of development as you have people who once had water supply in their homes no longer have it.

Some generations in the country have not had the benefit of having drinking water supplied by the state.

Figure 7.5: Water Project in Kogi State (Source: YouTube)

The water project shown above is a typical example of how politicians short-change Nigerians by providing substandard facilities. The project was ceremoniously declared open by officials. An attempt to show they are meeting the needs of local communities. No provision is made for its maintenance or source of continuous water supply needed. It gives the impression that water is free for the public. No proper drainage for the wastewater nor a befitting surrounding. It is served by an overhead tank supported by a crude pipe that will give after a few years. The aftermath of such projects is shown in the figure below.

Figure 7.6: Failed Water Project 1
(Source: Michael April 2023)

Figure 7.7: Failed Water Project 2
(Source: Michael April 2023)

It is evident that resources have been wasted on the projects. The problem of water scarcity in the communities remains.

AGRICULTURAL PRODUCTION

Nigeria should be able to feed itself as it is blessed with both land and sea. The efforts being made to support farmers should be lauded. Nigeria remains largely primarily a producer of raw material with little development in processing or even the storage of farm produce. The country still suffers from glut and high wastage during the harvest of many agricultural products. The reverse scarcity during the growing period and hence, higher prices.

It is documented that many cargo ships that come in fully loaded on arrival leave the Nigerian ports with little or no cargo. This supports the notion that the country does not produce enough to leave room for export. The little produced is not well managed, and no logistics in place to get the good harvest to where needed to reduce glut and wastage. There is the opportunity to put basic food preservation techniques such as canning into practice. Investors should consider building dedicated food storage facilities to help regulate the supply of agricultural produce.

The world experienced grain shortages in the first few months of the unfortunate war in Ukraine when ships were not allowed out of its ports. This is a story of a nation feeding its people and those of the world.

There is also the scope to add value to farm products like maize, cassava, and other starchy root crops. Starch for the pharmaceutical industry can be extracted, and the waste can be used for animal feeds. By so doing, employment is created, foreign exchange can be earned or a decrease in the importation of this product.

There is clearly an opportunity for the country to earn foreign exchange if more farm produce is sold to the international markets in different forms. It will also reduce wastage and enhance the continuity of service. An example of how everyone can benefit from farm produce is given below.

Figure 7.8: Yorkshire Bettys
(Source: Bettys' Customer's Standard Carrier Bag)

"A long time has passed since the first Bettys opened in 1919, but in many ways, Bettys is just the same. We still think that traditional ways are the best, that a beautiful setting is good for the soul, and that simple pleasures can improve life. Our purpose is to create treasured memories – we hope we can make one for you. We change our menus with the seasons, making the most of the freshest produce and, wherever possible, sourcing from farmers right here on our doorstep in Yorkshire."

How has this company managed to thrive over the years? This has happened due to having succeeding, committed, good management teams who share and sustain the founders' vision. They create treasured memory for each visitor, that is, each customer. Following the good experience, and the service received, they are recommended to friends and families. Bettys is a must-visit for anyone in Yorkshire.

The case study above has provided steady employment for many, steady and reliable purchases of products and services from its suppliers.

The situation in Nigeria is summarised by the caption in the figure below.

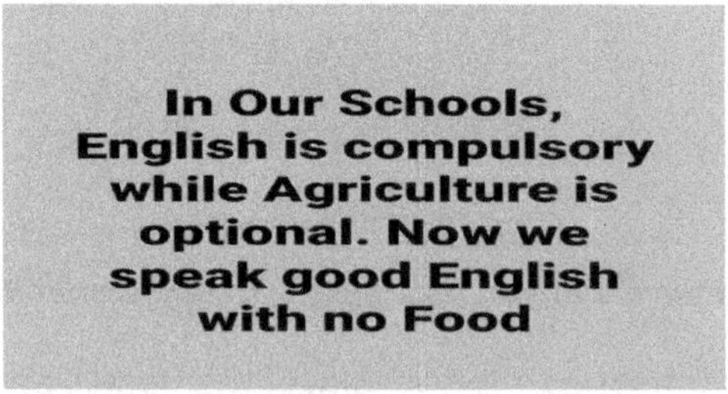

In Our Schools, English is compulsory while Agriculture is optional. Now we speak good English with no Food

Figure 7.9: Learning English without Food
(source: The Good Life, Facebook)

Figure 7.9 highlights that English is a taught language in Nigeria that will never and should never replace indigenous mother-tongue languages in the country. Pride must be seen in speaking fluently in one's native language.

Authors and speakers must take this into account when addressing Nigerians. It is natural for the brain to translate any information to the first language before processing. The result is also in the first language before being uttered to the audience in a common language that may differ from the native language.

The above advice is for everyone to write and speak simply to ensure understanding and assimilation. Speech writers should also take into account the people that will be reading their write-up. Officials that will be presenting a document prepared for them should ensure they have gone through it at least once before facing their live audience.

A piece of work requiring another reference, such as a dictionary for comprehension, will appeal to fewer people. It explains why some people start reading a book and never finish it or abandon it after the first few pages.

The English language is the business language in Nigeria. It allows all the people of Nigeria to carry out day-to-day transactions amongst themselves and others worldwide. It must be seen solely as so and not as a measure of intelligence. No one should be made to feel embarrassed or ridiculed for not being fluent in their command of the English language. Some English people cannot read or write English and are not embarrassed in any way. A caring society accommodates everyone immaterial of their circumstances.

Making English language study compulsory in Nigerian schools is commendable to allow everyone to have a basic command of the language. The educational system should also review the other needs of the nation. One significant need is food.

There is a need of refocussing academicians, students and everyone to acquire the knowledge and skills to produce more food to meet the increasing food requirement of the nation. The country's people should be educated on the importance of food production at all levels and proportions. Pride must be restored in farming and food production in general.

It is said that once food is available, the rest of people's needs are manageable. There is no better way than providing food for the government and leaders of Nigeria to display their passion for Nigerians. They should take every step or pronouncement that will make everyone, locally and internationally, feel that providing food for the masses is a top priority.

Farming is the profession of our land. The one that does not work will steal. Education without the hoe and cutlass is incomplete. It is incomplete. This is a popular song by school pupils during the march past in schools in some parts of Nigeria. The farmer harvest what was sowed many days before the harvest, so it is for Nigerians in the treatment of Nigerians by Nigerians.

Nigerian farmers at all levels must be supported by the government at all levels to be able to do their job freely. The government should come to their aid during natural disasters such as adverse weather conditions. The government has the duty to provide safe farming in all parts of the country. Everyone must be treated fairly, as no sector is more important than the other. No sector should be a threat to another, and the government should be seen to be able to support this.

There will be food shortages if farmers are unable to go to their farms due to fear for their lives. This should not be allowed; any identified threat should be dealt with severely so that it does not reappear in any part of the country.

Figure 7.10: Groundnut pyramids
(Source: Connect Nigeria)

Questions:

1. What happened to Nigerian groundnut pyramids?

2. What can lead to a farmer being scared to go to the farm?

3. Why is poultry farming as important as tomato farming?

4. How can the government support Nigerian Farmers?

5. What are the problems faced by Nigerian farmers?

Case Study: Choose a farm produce that production can be increased to meet local needs and then export. Explain why the product is not currently exported. Highlight four possible international markets and how each market can be reached. Also, give a detailed list of possible by-products and uses of the produce.

HYDROCARBON RESERVE

Nigeria is fortunate to be blessed with vast crude oil reserves. The discovery of oil was a blessing for the Nation. Unfortunately, the wealth from this liquid gold has been poorly managed. Refineries were built at the onset of oil discovery but have become obsolete repeatedly due to bad management by the Nigerian National Petroleum Corporation. It has not only run down its assets but got some of its prominent and iconic offices gutted by fire. The fire burnt very important data, information and historical records.

The refineries were poorly maintained and not upgraded. The nation export crude oil and import refined products at a loss. Hence, need for a foreign reserve to subsidise the importation of refined petroleum products.

What is amazing about this is the fact that the Nigeria National Petroleum Corporation (NNPC), the president and all legislative organs of the nation fail to address the absurdity of Nigeria not producing refined petroleum products locally.

The government and the agencies spend time and money squabbling over the amount of subsidy for petroleum products and how to source its funding. It can only be described as the product lack of foresight and corruption by corrupt decision-makers who do not think of how to positively put an end to this drain on the wealth of Nigeria.

Well-managed oil corporations worldwide declared record profits year after, albeit for occasional major disasters. The Ukrainian war (2022) saw increased profits by those corporations, while NNPC, which controls a fair amount of petroleum, cannot make petroleum products available in Nigeria. It was not able to take on new opportunities that became available.

National interest is putting competent people in key positions in the country's establishments to work in the interest of the nation's people. The nation and the people of Nigeria will benefit much better if competent people are in place to run the NNPC. History shows that the corporation performed well once before recent underperformance. The fact that there is no visible improvement in NNPC's efforts to make available all year the necessary petroleum products.

There is nothing new under the sun, just as many nations worldwide are doing very well with their crude oil. In the nation's interest, the Nigerian government should find out what the other successful oil-producing nations have done with their liquid gold.

Competent management should be looking at and putting into place logistics to ensure that there are petroleum products in the country at any time of the year. Inventory level and consumption rate are available to work with. The data should be made available to the public. This will reassure the people, ending panic and chaos associated with news that causes sporadic scarcity in the country.

Nigeria may need to think out of the box by considering the idea of having a foreign chief executive for the NNPC. This person will be given the mandate to maximise the corporation's assets. The merit of this is the removal of ethnic sentiments, which has crippled NNPC.

Developed nations make it crystal clear they want the from anywhere in the world. They do not shy away from appointing competent executives to run their national establishments like their central bank, football federation or railways, to name a few. Competent professionals do not work for money but for the good of the organisation; they manage solely because they know they will be rewarded adequately for both success and failure. They do all they can to succeed to be able to retain their role or be headhunted by another establishment.

A simple engine search on the internet will list a catalogue of disasters linked to petroleum that has engulfed Nigeria.

Some examples are given below:

Fire on southeast Nigerian state oil pipeline kills 16 peoplehttps://www.reuters.com › article.

12 Oct 2018 – Sixteen people were **killed** after a **fire** broke out on Friday on an oil pipeline in the southeast of Nigeria, a spokesman for the Nigerian ...Missing: ~~office~~ ▯| Must include: office

Abuja Conoil fire: NNPC allay fears about safety of its building

https://www.premiumtimesng.com › news › 150927-up...

5 Dec 2013 – The **fire** broke out when a fuel tanker offloaded petrol at the filling station across the road, opposite the **NNPC Towers**. There was ...

Three killed, 10 vehicles burnt as fire guts NNPC filling station

https://www.premiumtimesng.com › news › more-news

24 Apr 2016 – Three people **died** Saturday, and 10 vehicles burnt at a filling station belonging to the state-owned Nigeria National Petroleum Corporation ...

Nigeria: Fire Guts NNPC Lagos Office - allAfrica.com

https://allafrica.com › stories

25 Dec 2002 – No **life** was **lost** as workers and visitors to the strategic **office** turned up for the day›s business only to find the **building** in ...

Fire NNPC GMD now for insensitivity, Niger Delta youths tell ...https://www.vanguardngr.com › News

21 Sept 2017 – –-Says 10,000 youths have **lost** their jobs. By Johnbosco Agbakwuru. ABUJ - NIGER Delta Youth Leaders has told President Muhammadu Buhari to.

Fire guts down NNPC depot in Suleja - Vanguard News

https://www.vanguardngr.com › News

29 Jan 2017 – A Petrol tanker on **fire**. "An articulated vehicle was burnt while the loading canopy and some pipes were damaged. No **life** was, however, **lost** ...

N556bn crude oil lost to vandalism, others in three months https://punchng.com › n556bn-crude-oil-lost-to-vandali...

27 Dec 2021 – On some incidents that led to the crude oil **losses** in September, the **NNPC** stated that "production (was) curtailed due to pipeline ...

Figure 7.11: Scenes of Petroleum Related Disaster in Nigeria (Source: Google Search)

Figure 7.12: Scenes of Petroleum-Related Disaster in Nigeria (i) (Source: Google Search)

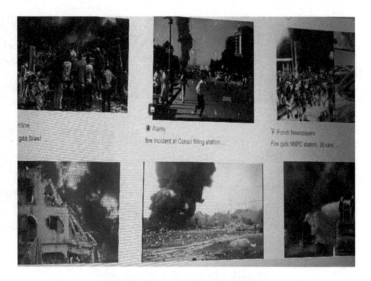

Figure 7.13: Scenes of Petroleum Related Disaster in
Nigeria(ii) (Source: Google Search)

NNPC should be responsible for setting standards for the safe transportation of petroleum products nationwide. Time and time again, there is yet another incident of a tanker with tons of flammable product involved in a road incident. The aftermath is always lost properties, severe environmental damage and, in many cases, loss of lives.

Figure 7.14: A Good Petrol Tanker in Nigeria (Source: Photos by the author April 2023)

It will be good for NNPC to start recording and keeping records of such incidents. Data such as type, age, of the truck, owner of the truck, insurers, and date the truck was last tested for roadworthiness should be captured. The quantity of the product lost should also be recorded. The number of life lost must be recorded as well. All other resulting losses like houses, motorcycles, and vehicles from each incident should be recorded with fair monetary value.

The loss of a tanker en route does not only cause severe damage at the incident scene. Many people would have been stuck on the road on the day of the incident. There is a consequent shortage of the products in the community it was destined for in the first instance. The road or bridge where it happened could be rendered impassable for weeks, thus causing immense inconveniences for its regular users.

It is time to stop dismissing serious and fatal incidents from petroleum-related incidents. Victims must be identified and adequately compensated from a fund set up for that purpose. Nigerians must no longer be made to bear the consequences of haulers who do not prioritise the safety of people and their assets.

Failure to have relevant data on the losses from these incidents does show that NNPC management and Nigerian leaders do not relate to them not to talk of thinking of stopping them. The lives lost are not recognised or accounted for, no compassion, no responsibility by anybody, no support for victims, and no reprimand for those at fault.

There should be a detailed report with a summary of each incident. There should be an independent victim support department that will enable those who have suffered losses to be able each person to resume normal life as much as possible. *Figure 7.15* is a Google search for the headline news about a man who died on the premises of a bank while trying to get some of his money from his account with the bank during the introduction of new Naira notes in January 2023.

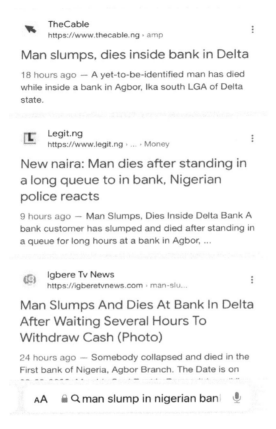

Figure 7.15: Sad Story of a Man Who Died in a Bank
(2023) (Source: Google Search)

Who is responsible for his death? What lead to his death? Why was he in the bank? Would he have gone to the bank if cash dispensers were doing what they are called? What happens to his money with the bank? Who will take care of the funeral? The questions are unending; if there is one, the Victim Support

Organisation has the task of asking and getting answers to the most relevant questions.

Should the case be that there is no Victim Support Organisation to speak and fight for ordinary Nigerians? It is the Duty of the government to support such organisations because they are never profit-making. They, however enrich the nation by stopping wealth burning and bringing relief to victims of a loss.

Nigerians should consider setting up their Victim Support Organisation if such is not forthcoming from the government. It will require professionals to offer their services voluntarily, initially for free, until the organisation is well established and in a position to get fee-paying clients. Some cases can be taken on a no-win no-fee basis. This is how to establish social justice in society and bring sanity into the judicial system as well.

A Victim Support Organisation gives a sense of hope to the hopeless and helps to avoid rip off by the establishment. It gives a voice to victims and a trusted advocate to go to. It creates a healthy society in that established bodies cannot act carelessly or as a bully because there is a price to pay for their failures.

RESOURCE MANAGEMENT

Nigeria has a landmass endowed with different resources. Its expanse allows the cultivation of a variety of agricultural products.

Its weather cum seasons vary from north to south, with temperate conditions in some areas. There is ample sunshine across the nation all year round that enables farming. It is not surprising that international interest in the nation is not declining. Table 3 below is a summary of resources known to be available in Nigeria.

Table 7.1: Natural Resources in Nigeria
(Source: Nigerian Embassy, Sweden)

S/N - State - Resources

S/N	State	Resources
1	Abia	Gold, Lead/Zinc, Limestone, Oil/Gas & Salt
2	Abuja	Cassiterite, Clay, Dolomite, Gold, Lead/Zinc, Marble & Tantalite
3	Adamawa	Bentonite, Gypsum, Kaolin & Magnesite
4	Akwa Ibom	Clay, Lead/Zinc, Lignite, Limestone, Oil/Gas, Salt & Uranium
5	Anambra	Clay, Glass-Sand, Gypsum, Iron-ore, Lead/Zinc, Lignite, Limestone, Phosphate & Salt
6	Bauchi	Gold, Cassiterite (tine ore), Columbite, Gypsum, Wolfram, Coal, Limestone, Lignite, Iron-ore & Clay
7	Bayelsa	Clay, Gypsum, Lead/Zinc, Lignite, Limestone, Manganese, Oil/Gas & Uranium
8	Benue	Barite, Clay, Coal, Gemstone, Gypsum, Iron-Ore, Lead/Zinc, Limestone, Marble & Salt
9	Borno	Bentonite, Clay, Diatomite, Gypsum, Hydro-carbon, Kaolin & Limestone
10	Delta	Clay, Glass-sand, Gypsum, Iron-ore, Kaolin, Lignite, Marble & Oil/Gas
11	Ebonyi	Gold, Lead/Zinc & Salt

12	Edo	Bitumen, Clay Dolomite, Phosphate, Glass-sand, Gold, Gypsum, Iron-ore, Lignite, Limestone, Marble & Oil/Gas
13	Ekiti	Feldspar, Granite, Kaolin, Syenite & Titanium
14	Enugu	Coal, Lead/Zinc & Limestone
15	Gombe	Gemstone & Gypsum
16	Imo	Gypsum, Lead/Zinc, Lignite, Limestone, Marcasite, Oil/Gas, Phosphate & Salt
17	Cross River	Barite, Lead/Zinc, Lignite, Limestone, Manganese, Oil/Gas, Salt & Uranium
18	Jigawa	Butyls
19	Kaduna	Amethyst, Aqua Marine, Asbestos, Clay, Gemstone, Gold, Graphite, Kaolin, Kyanite, Mica, Rock Crystal, Ruby, Sapphire, Se, Topaz & Tourmaline
20	Kano	Cassiterites, Copper, Gemstone, Glass-sand, Lead/Zinc, Pyrrocaine & Tantalite
21	Kastina	Kaolin, Marble & Salt
22	Kebbi	Gold
23	Kogi	Cole, Dolomite, Feldspar, Gypsium, Iron-ore, Kaolin, Marble, Talc & Tantalite
24	Kwara	Cassiterite, Columbite, Feldspar, Gold, Iron-ore, Marble, Mica & Tantalite
25	Lagos	Bitumen, Clay & Glass-sand
26	Nasarawa	Amethyst (Topaz Garnet), Barite, Chalcopyrite, Clay, Columbite, Coking Coal, Dolomite/Marble, Feldspar, Galena, Iron-ore, Limestone, Mica, Salt, Sapphire, Talc, Tantalite, Tourmaline Quartz
27	Niger	Gold, Lead/Zinc & Talc

28	Ogun	Bitumen, Clay, Feldspar, Gemstone, Kaolin, Limestone & Phosphate
29	Ondo	Bitumen, Clay, Coal, Dimension Stones, Feldspar, Gemstone, Glass-Sand, Granite, Gypsium, Kaolin, Limestone & Oil/Gas
30	Osun	Columbite, Gold, Granite, Talc, Tantalite & Tourmaline
31	Oyo	Aqua Marine, Cassiterite, Clay, Dolomite, Gemstone, Gold, Kaolin, Marble, Silimonite, Talc & Tantalite
32	Plateau	Barite, Bauxite, Bentonites, Bismuth, Cassiterite, Clay, Coal, Emerald, Fluoride, Gemstone, Granite, Iron-ore, Kaolin, Lead/Zinc, Marble, Molybdenite, Salt, Tantalite/Columbite, Tin & Wolfram
33	Rivers	Clay, Glass-Sand, Lignite, Marble & Oil/Gas
34	Sokoto	Clay, Flakes, Gold, Granite, Gypsum, Kaolin, Laterite, Limestone, Phosphate, Potash, Silica Sand & Salt
35	Taraba	Lead/Zinc
36	Yobe	Soda Ash
37	Zamfara	Coal, Cotton & Gold

"There are tremendous opportunities for investments in the solid mineral sector of the Nigerian economy. Prospecting licenses are granted by the Federal Ministry of Solid Minerals Development to investors (local and foreign), to enable them to participate in the exploitation of the vast mineral resources in Nigeria. Source: Nigeria Embassy, Stockholm, Sweden"

QUESTIONS:

1. What are the natural resources in your locality?

2. Are there any noticeable activities to extract a natural resource in your locality, or is it being extracted already?

3. Which companies are extracting any identified natural resources in Nigeria?

4. How easy is it for people to know about the resources in their locality and where relevant documentation will be found in Nigeria?

A THEORY FOR THE NIGERIAN PETROLEUM CORPORATION

The theory is that Nigeria and Nigerians would have fared much better if the NNPC, the whole crude oil and associated resources in Nigeria were owned by one family. This conclusion is arrived at following a review of successful organisations. The leader has a vision for growth and takes pride in the business. The organisation has a face loved by the people, and there is a long-term established good reputation and history of good leadership. The vision of the founder is carried on from one generation to another. Recruitment is competitive and successful candidates become committed to the organisation's vision by taking ownership of the family. So, the vision continues.

A successful corporation goes into strategic alliances with partners and other stakeholders. Their positive impact is felt and enjoyed in society. The organisation grows and grows the people as well. Its products and services are readily available to the delight of everyone.

A family-owned NNPC would be caring for the communities where it operates and the wider society. NNPC staff and managers should see the corporation as theirs while working there so its future success and growth would be a vision for all, including all Nigerians who should enjoy its product and services.

No family company burns its wealth like the NNPC has been burning for the last few years. There should be no fuel scarcity anytime in Nigeria with NNPC's resources. A family-run organisation in the position of NNPC will operate an inventory level with trigger levels and action plans to ensure demand is met all year round without interruption.

Nigeria should not be importing petroleum products at the level it is doing. Nigeria should not borrow money externally from lenders such as the International Monetary Fund (IMF) or use its foreign reserves to subsidise the importation of petroleum products.

The same principle can be applied to other national organisations like the Nigerian Ports Authority (NPA).

QUESTIONS:

1. How is Nigerian wealth burnt by the NPA?

2. How will you describe how NNPC is being managed?

3. Why can Nigeria thrive solely on NNPC's resources?

4. List five other natural resources extracted in Nigeria and their roles in the world?

5. How efficiently are Nigerian natural resources being managed to benefit the country?

6. Why can't the NNPC produce sufficient basic petroleum products for Nigerians?

7. Should Nigeria be importing petroleum products?

8. Why do you think NNPC is failing the nation in making available petroleum products as needed in Nigeria?

8

NIGERIAN SCORECARD

Nigerians should rate those in place of authority because they need to know how they perform. This should be done at all levels of government; it can also be done for various sectors of the Nigerian economy.

Table 8.1: The Score Card

NIGERIAN SCORECARD		
National	**Yes/No**	
State		
Local Govt		
Please circle as relevant for National rating and national institutions. Give the name of the state and local government as applicable.		
Social Need	**Summary** **(same, better or worse)**	**Mark (1 to 10)**
Accountability		
Education		
Electricity		
Employment		
Hospital		
Justice		
Policing		
Roads		
Tourism		
Water		
Total		
Conclusion		
Date		

Table 8.1 above is a template that can be adapted as relevant. The summary column will have one of three possible outcomes: (1) Same, (2) Better and (3) Worse. This is in comparison to the previous assessment. The frequency of assessment should be agreed upon and fixed. Mark will be up to ten for each social need. The conclusion will be used to state the social need that is need of most urgent attention.

The scorecard will act as feedback to leaders and decision-makers. It will assist in evaluating progress and planning what the public wants to see done. Anyone can complete the scorecard for any organisation to get their message to decision-makers. Researchers and consultants can use it to survey a prescribed population because anonymity allows the free expression of views. No name is required to enable fair and true feedback.

The scorecard can easily be made to rate the state of the petroleum industry in Nigeria. Any government that imports petrol can be scored as failing Nigerians. This can be said of the management of the NNPC. It will then be seen how an aspiring politician will tell the people of their intention to continue the policies of a failed government.

ENERGY CONSPIRACY IN NIGERIA

There is the conspiracy theory that people behind diesel, petrol and generators work to sabotage efforts made by the government for the nation to have a regular supply of electricity. It is hard to understand this theory. The consistent failure of each government in Nigeria to address intermittent or non-existent electricity is solely due to unacceptable bad management and corruption by all involved.

Bad management is the fact that the players in the electricity supply, the National Electric Power Authority (NEPA) in particular, failed to upgrade and put in place a culture of gradual increase in power generation. It was sad to live with a system that saw the availability of electricity decreasing every year rather than increasing. It should be highlighted that many manufacturers had to close and leave Nigeria. Hospitals and those that cannot leave the country must invest heavily in their own power generation. People's lives are daily put at risk as a result.

The failure of both the government and what became of the National Electric Power Authority (NEPA) to address this is callous and a great disservice to the nation. The government's privatisation of the generation and distribution of electricity in the country has seen little improvement. The private companies claim the government is stifling their efforts. Nigerians have to pay for electric poles, metre, and connections to get connected. However, the pole and metre belong to the electricity provider, a rip-off of Nigerians.

The role of corruption is equally obvious in the amount of money each government from the 1970s has spent on power provision. The fact is that the more money made available, the less power generated or available to the people. Each government claims to spend more on power generation. But no account is ever given; painfully, it is business as usual. Whatever happened to all the money is never questioned by government auditors who have lost their reputation as they have certified colossal mismanagement and are deemed part of corrupt practices in the system.

Those making money because of poor power supply and stemming their efforts to keep the status quo must have a myopic view stemming from greed and selfishness. They stifle creativity and development as they lack national interest in their deeds. They do not think of leaving a positive legacy for future generations.

They also fail to acknowledge the loss of lives and assets lost resulting from the poor power supply in the country. While the generator, diesel/petrol dealers make money due to poor power supply, the people lose hard-earned money by burning fuel and maintaining generators.

It is unclear why the government has not created an environment for international players who would effectively manage investment in power generation. They will provide the service the people deserve and, in the process, make their money. This will result in a win-win situation for the populace, and the industry, increasing employment and reducing poverty for many.

QUESTIONS:

1. What impact will having enough electric supply have on the sale of generations?

2. What are the different places that use generators even when there is enough electricity supply?

3. Will it ever be possible not to use generators in Nigeria, and why?

4. Why should diesel and generator marketers be concerned with increasing the electricity supply in Nigeria?

5. How does the high rate of diesel consumption in Nigeria affect the environment?

CHAPTER

HEALTH

Countless Nigerians have died because of poor medical treatment. Poor medical facilities remain visible at all levels across Nigeria. Where there is a form of care, the cost is off-putting for many Nigerians. Even the rich fail to get proper medical care in the country. Therefore, It is not surprising that its president at one time openly goes abroad for medical check-ups and care.

Malaria, often resulting from mosquito bites, stands out as the cause of death for many Nigerians. Researchers have not found a vaccination for the disease.

In addition to the number of lives lost, billions of naira are spent annually on the treatment of malaria. Nigerians also spend billions of naira on sprays to combat mosquitoes in homes and offices as a step to kill them. This is in addition to investments in other defensive installations, such as nets on windows and beds to keep mosquitos at bay.

Figure 9.1: Netted Bed t Keep Mosquito Away
(Source: Michael April 2023)

Figure 9.2: Sample Insect Killer Sprays
(Source: Micheal April 2023)

The federal and some state governments budget for mosquito nets. The funding allocated for mosquito nets, as in many other projects in Nigeria, does not serve the earmarked purpose. Cases of the purchase of substandard and ineffective mosquito nets are easily available by a simple search on the internet. Some Nigerian leaders are thereby taking advantage of the health issues caused by mosquitoes to defraud its citizens.

It is obvious that mosquito is a menace and drains the resources endowed in Nigeria. It is a hole that must be plugged. Mosquitoes are, therefore, a common enemy to all Nigerians that should be fought every day. Young and adults alike have to understand their role in the battle.

The most effective action to prevent being beaten by mosquitoes is to prevent their existence where possible and make their reproduction as difficult as possible.

The End Malaria Council in Nigeria should be more visible in the country and take the front row in the crusade to reduce the number of harmful mosquitos at any point in time.

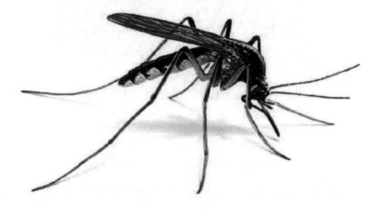

Figure 9.3: The Mosquito

How can Nigeria prevent its citizens from this insect? There must be a push to eradicate mosquitoes through actions that make it difficult for their reproduction. Mosquitoes thrive in stagnant water. Nigeria Public Health should have this as the number one priority and have the whole nation well-informed in ensuring that no stagnant water is available for the condition favourable to mosquitos' incubation.

Figure 9.4: Stagnant Water for Incubation of Mosquito
(Source: Michael April 2023)

Nigerians have for long enhanced the massive reproduction of mosquitoes to their own detriment. Conducive conditions are provided in the way water is made available in the house and in the method of disposing of domestic water and sewage. Each house is likely to have septic and water tanks. This means such a house is unknowingly producing mosquitoes. House owners should invest in airtight tanks where one is needed for water storage. The traditional septic tank, otherwise referred to as a soakaway pit, should ideally have a vent taller than the highest point on the roof of the house.

This will take the odour away and deter mosquito breeding in the pit.

The task here is for every Nigerian to see every stagnant water as a mosquito breeding spot. Everyone, young and old, should commit to disposing of any stagnant water they come across wherever possible. There should be a regular schedule aimed at disposing of stagnant water. This should not be limited to domestic buildings; offices and all installations should be made to do this.

Institutions such as hospitals should be made to have an annual inspection of their grounds for stagnant water and report and recommend actions to reduce incidences of stagnant water. It will be assuring for the public to know that their hospitals are mosquito free.

Housing estates, barracks of the military forces, police and government agencies that provide housing should be included in areas that should inspect and report with recommendations on what needs to be done to eradicate stagnant water.

The slogan: **"No stagnant water"** should be a watermark on some public health stationeries. The public at large should not only embrace it but also put it into practice by not walking past stagnant water. They should pause and take a moment to see if they can do anything to dispose of the water. Bottles, cans or water-holding containers should not be left on the streets. This means the era of throwing such items out on the streets should end.

The local councils should see to it that waterways are in continuous flow. Necessary investment should not be spared or diverted to achieve the desired objective of eliminating mosquito breeding spots.

Water in potholes and flooded roads will continue to pose a challenge for the nation. There is bound to be an improvement over time in dealing with potholes and flooded roads as the important role of safe and dry roads in reducing mosquito breeding is acknowledged.

Health is wealth, so there is the cry for improved health service provision to save lives and time people spend in hospitals. The situation where a family member must be present in the hospital to provide care for their relative is a drain on resources. Such carers run the risk of getting an infection which could take them out for a while.

Questions:

1. What can be done to reduce the incidence of malaria resulting from mosquito bites?

2. Why are there no mosquitoes on Disney Land grounds in the different parts of the world?

3. How can the person on the street contribute to the quest to reduce the mosquito population?

4. What actions is the Ministry of Health taking to combat malaria in Nigeria?

5. How is the mosquito burning the wealth of Nigeria?

CHAPTER

10

WEALTH CREATION

ealth creation is simply the addition of value to a product or provision of service that enables an increase in asset or wealth. It can also be achieved by the monetisation of intellectual property. The receipt of royalty is a classic example, as this can be in perpetuity. This means that royalty continues after the death of the originator. The singer and writer, Dolly Parton, has received royalty payments for using her songs in films and allowing other artists to reproduce them.

Small businesses are usually the backbone of a successful national economy. Small businesses are unable to thrive in Nigeria because of high running costs. Each one virtually must make provisions for water, electricity and transportation. Where they can put these basics in place, moving their goods and services around the country is made almost impossible by the poor road networks in the country.

Having access to credit is key to wealth creation. Money is needed when a project is undergoing development and testing as well as for initial marketing. Some products still fail even after being introduced to the market. Organisations and entrepreneurs need finance for research and development that creates wealth.

Some institutions exist to provide financial backing to developers and creative start-ups. It may be difficult to get the backing needed from these institutions and banks. This is because a form of security will be required to guarantee payment of their money. Many start-up entrepreneurs, therefore, resort to seeking financial support from peers and family members.

The non-repayment of financial support by borrowers should be highlighted as a major barrier to wealth creation in Nigeria. The win-win situation expected when a loan is taken for, say to buy a vehicle is what should result when finance is sought for wealth creation. The borrower buys and owns the vehicle, and the lender gets their money back with interest. Hence, both parties are better off because of the transaction.

However, many peer-to-peer deals fail, resulting in a loss of wealth by the lending peer. In other cases, the lender and borrower suffer losses with varying consequences. There is usually a breakdown in cordial relationships and stress which may lead to high blood pressure, heart attacks, and lawsuits.

Access to credit starts with the borrower summoning the courage to approach the lender. The motive of the borrower, however, cannot be ascertained by the lender, who will normally act in good faith and trust as no security is put in place.

On the other end of the phone line was a borrower mixing sobbing with the story of seeking financial assistance to pay for repairs needed on a rented property. The Council could take over the property if the required repairs are not carried out within a specified time. The borrower was calmed down and assured there would be no property loss.

The lender could provide the money from available funds earmarked for another project. The conversation continued. How much are you looking to borrow? "One thousand five hundred pounds," came the response. The borrower also added that the money would be repaid in two instalments. The first payment was agreed to pay a month after the date of the money transfer. The money was sent immediately to complete the work without further delay.

The borrower defaulted and repaid two hundred and fifty pounds of the money about six months later. The balance was never paid back or spoken about.

Here is an example of how a credit-providing body is left to bear the consequences. The money was, of course, needed for the original purpose for which it was earmarked. As it has been spent (loaned out), a credit card was called upon to pay the contractor doing the extension work when the necessary payment was due. The following questions should be considered.

1. Why was the money not repaid by the borrower?

2. What would have happened if the lender did not have the means to pay their contractor?

3. What do you think happened to the relationship between the lender and borrower?

4. What should the borrower do even if the borrower cannot repay the loan?

5. What would you do if faced with a similar situation today?

Nigerians who seek credit should have the mentality to repay what is borrowed for mutual benefit in the long run. It follows the basic principle of repeat patronage of good service. A borrower that repays can go back to the same lender to seek credit. The reward is what is termed a good credit rating. Other lenders use the rating to determine whether to lend to a new client. On a person-to-person level, better relationship, trust and credibility is developed when a borrower repays.

FOOD PROCESSING AND PACKAGING

Nigeria should increase the value of its natural resources by processing them. Raw materials like cocoa beans, coffee beans, and cassava tubers are bought in tonnes. At the same time, the finished products are sold in grams, just as crude oil is sold in barrels and derived products are bought in litres.

It has been suggested that sellers of electricity generators and diesel are colluding to see to it that the nation does not have a constant supply of electricity. While this might be upheld to some extent, there is the overwhelming failure of the government to ensure there is a functional national grid. That is the supply line that all houses and businesses in cities and towns can be connected to when ready to become a customer.

The level of theft from the little electricity supplied cannot be ignored. There are millions of users not legally connected to the grid, by so doing, use unmetered electricity. This is theft that should be widely discouraged.

There is also the issue of non-payment by legally connected customers. Some simply due to their powerful position in the country. A failure to show a good example for others to follow.

Nigerians are indeed ready to pay for electricity if it is provided. This is evident in the fact that they can and have been buying diesel/petrol to run generators. Some for twenty-four hours of the day and seven days of the week all year round. Some now have more than one generator for their comfort.

When a leader goes astray, the people being led consequently go astray as well. This has been the journey of Nigeria for a long time, leaders leading the people astray. Corrupt leaders leading their people in corruption.

Case Study: How much has been returned to Nigeria from abroad as part of the money a previous leader named Abacha took out of Nigeria?

Questions:

1. How can Nigeria stop its leaders from high-level corruption?

2. Do the armed forces, including the police, pay for electricity in Nigeria? List where you think these bodies use electricity and discuss the impact of their payment or no payment on the energy companies.

3. Why do Nigerian leaders steal the country's money in colossal amounts to take a different country?

4. What checks and balances would you put in place to stop the laundering of Nigerian money by its own leaders?

DIASPORA NIGERIANS

Nigerians abroad are referred to as being in the diaspora while non-African-looking non-Nigerians in Nigeria are seen as expatriates. Expatriates and diasporas are the same as they are both in another country for one reason or the other. Many diasporas or expatriates look forward to going back to their countries, while some never want to.

Many Nigerians in the diaspora not only wish to come back to Nigeria but also to see the country's resources manged much better for the people's interest. They want to see improvement in the facilities in the hospitals, schools, offices and the general living standards of all Nigerians. Their passion for the country is difficult to kill. For this reason, they do all they can and are allowed to do as their contribution to make Nigeria a better place to live.

Nigerians in the diaspora should be taking their colleagues, friends, and families on holiday visits to Nigeria. They should recommend Nigeria as a place for people to visit, work or invest in. Those who want to do take up the opportunities offered in Nigeria. This is a reason for an increase in expatriates in the country.

Many Nigerians in the diaspora who wish and have tried to invest in Nigeria have been frustrated in many ways. This has been touched a little bit earlier. Their attempt and efforts to create wealth in Nigeria have been made to face the utmost difficulties resulting from the failure of those on the ground in Nigeria. They fail to see the bigger picture; they believe they are taking advantage of the physical absence of those in the diaspora. They run many businesses aground to the loss of all concerned and Nigeria as a whole.

The story of the Nigerian baker in Canada mentioned before is a good example of how a diaspora Nigerian can create wealth in Nigeria. He has the template for successfully replicating his bakery in different locations. He does not and cannot be at the different sites simultaneously but has trusted hard-working staff who ensure the smooth operations of each site.

Nigerians in Nigeria must now support their fellow Nigerians in the diaspora who attempts to invest in them in Nigeria to create wealth for all through gainful employment and development of individuals for a better tomorrow.

Questions:

1. What are the barriers a diaspora entrepreneur faces in Nigeria wishing to run a business?

2. How does it benefit Nigerians to look after the interest of diasporas?

3. Why do diasporas desire to invest in Nigeria?

4. With examples, what is meant by a win-win situation, and how can this stop wealth burning in Nigeria?

CHAPTER

11

ONE NATION

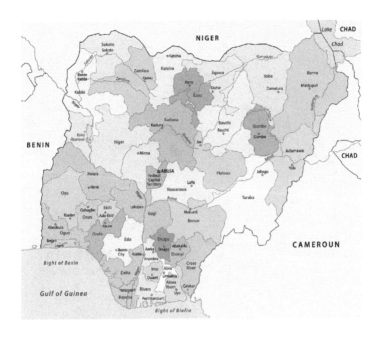

Figure 11.1: States of Nigeria (Source: uk.images)

Nigeria is made up of many ethnic groups, and some have agitated for the separation of the country. This raises questions about how many parts the country should be split into and where the boundaries will be. Another important question is how long it would take before the quest for further separation is birthed and agitated.

Figure 11.2: Peoples of Nigeria (Source: Uk.images)

The counter-resistance to keep the country as one nation is in the heat of the debate and agitation for separation. There is strength in the number and the variety of cultures to be enjoyed by all if one nation can be sustained.

There needs to be a paradigm change amongst those in Nigeria who abuse their power to create disunity amongst the different people in the country. There should be no case for tribal war in Nigeria in 2022. This is not yet the case; people are still fighting one another for territorial supremacy and ownership.

The situation in Nigeria can be described as being in middle age crisis. It has different ethnic groups yet to see and treat themselves as people of one nation. The earlier this is addressed, the earlier the nation will be seen as being progressive. Each citizen is likely to have a time of middle age crisis. Surviving it requires early identification of stress factors. This can include perceived success or failure in a career, loss of key providers, high financial gearing, peer pressure, shady deals coming to light, or becoming burnout. The list of factors that can lead to a stressful life is inexhaustible. One should be conscious of their circumstances to successfully manage that stage in life.

The best way to get over the pain suffered by the different peoples of Nigeria is to use the very little they get from the government to foster their development. The little available should be best used to foster their own progress rather than devoting them to bringing down opponents. This is what successful organisations do, focus on their visions, maximising resources for positive growth. It should be highlighted that organisations that work to bring down their competitors usually collapse or end up being taken over.

Nigeria has enough landmass and diverse natural resources to cater to and accommodate everyone. National and State governments should be working together in the provision of accommodation for people to settle into. New towns and villages can be created to alleviate tensions caused by the scramble for and grabbing of arable land.

The visible action of the government at all levels to act in the interest of one nation will galvanise the importantly needed sense of collective ownership and oneness. The elimination of lobsided appointments and having one policy for the nation. The transparent location of an industry based on economics is one example. Having open public consultations on key national matters will see people across the nation working together to achieve a common goal.

This is because there is a school of thought stating that current Nigeria is not a nation based on the history of how it came to being and how it is being run. This book is not to debunk or agree with. It is however evident that there is no unifying common interest in the populace which is important in driving a nation forward.

The Federal government that pursues orderliness, justice, and truth will see this transcending to state and local governments. The people will respond positively to such a government.

The issue of a unifying business language is essential for a nation. English has, by default, become that language for Nigeria. This does not mean local languages should become inferior but should be recognised. People must have pride in their mother tongue or first language.

There has been a failed project to create a new language called WaZoBia by combining the three main languages in Nigeria. It is a victim of a lack of continuity in policies of one government to another. The project was not made a core subject in the educational system to be taught yearly or taken on by the populace.

It is proposed here that rather than creating a new language, resources should be made available so that at the national level, all documents are available in Hausa, Ibo, and Yoruba. Each state should have documents in one of the three languages related to it. Pride should be taken in airing news in local dialects. This is done all over the world.

The educational system has a role in creating fluidity on the language issue. This can be achieved by making it part of the curriculum for every child to learn one of the three main languages at a point in time before leaving secondary school. This will equally enhance community cohesion as people can communicate with each other's language. People will also feel relaxed and comfortable with one another as they can interact socially and on business levels.

Moving and settling in different parts of the country will happen with less anxiety about the local language as more people understand and speak a second Nigerian language. There will be more use of each Hausa, Igbo, and Yoruba language across the country. There will be mutual respect among the people as language becomes less of a barrier to interacting with each other.

Book publishers, authors, and writers' role is to make more books and educational publications available in the Nigerian language. International researchers will be attracted to Nigeria with the availability of more educational materials in the local language.

Integration and total unity of all the people in the country are needed for a nation to develop. A sense of belonging, ownership, and affinity for the whole land, with every citizen respecting one another, will produce an equitable society. There will be less striving for calls for division and separation. Every Nigerian should be free, comfortable as well as confident to move around in the country.

The practice of rotation of where the president comes from should be discounted as this will never produce the best leader for the country. The current practice appears to rule out a female president in Nigeria for generations.

The south-north presidential rotational practice has shown a lack of continuation of policies and developments from one government to another. It also continues to enshrine ethnic division, as noted in biased appointments made by each government. The country suffers again in not getting the best candidates to run its different departments as they are filled with less competent people solely due to ethnicity. The public knowledge of their non-competitive selection erodes their authority and ability to perform. This is the vicious cycle the citizens of Nigeria must put a stop to.

It has been shown that the separation of the people of Nigeria will not unite all the different ethnic groups that make up the country. The kingmakers of the country must therefore put the interest of all Nigerians first. They now need to allow a process where the most capable and qualified person is elected as the president of the country.

The selection process and the decision-makers should be made public. This transparency will give credence to the leaders that come out of the process. Those involved in the selection process will command the respect of the highest order for being responsible for selecting good leaders for the nation. They would be seen as nationalists having followers that have the same national interest.

Questions:

1. Who are the kingmakers in Nigeria, and what role have they in unifying the populace?

2. How do you create a new community that reflects the people of Nigeria?

3. What do you understand by a common goal, and state why it is essential for development?

4. How will the kingmakers know that their actions are destroying the country?

5. Why is it important to encourage the use of one's mother tongue language?

PATRIOTISM

How patriotic are the people of Nigeria? This is difficult to answer because, as highlighted earlier, there is no unifying interest or vision for the people of Nigeria. A leader with a vision passionately pursues it and leaves a legacy behind. A vision that is in the interest of society will enthuse high positive expectations and will be bought by the populace. It can become a national goal as pride and achievement are associated with it.

Figure 11.3: The Jollof Rice

The Nigerian Jollof rice has gained international recognition. This is so because Nigerians have been successful in making people around the world enjoy it. Passion and love for what is Nigerian are essential for the country's development.

The practice of politicians and kingmakers holding meetings abroad should be discouraged. This shows a lack of passion for what is available in Nigeria just as many Nigerians crave anything made outside the Country.

There are many suitable venues in the country where such meetings should be taking place in the future. It will not only help the local economy but also show the readiness to associate with that which is Nigerian.

The question must be asked of the leaders of the oath taken to defend the integrity of Nigeria.

A patriotic leader should enthuse passion in doing what is in the best interest of all Nigerians rather than be regionally obsessed. Loyalty and trust are lost once this characteristic is seen in a leader.

The late Queen Elizabeth II of the United Kingdom was attributed to being a dedicated leader that won the love of many within the country and all around the world. She was patriotic and served the nation until her death at the good old age of 96 years. Floral tributes came from across the world from the announcement of her death. She was accorded a state funeral where world leaders congregated in London to say farewell to her. Only six nations were not officially invited.

Figure 11.4: Floral Tribute, Green Park, London

The question is which Nigerian leader has served passionately to deserve a state funeral. This will be a tall order as none has made any remarkable positive mark in its history.

The recent breed of Nigerian leaders has to retune their understanding of leadership and put the people they lead first. The leader will be well looked after in the pursuit of the welfare of its people. A leader seen to be serving Nigerians will be served accordingly by the same Nigerians. Everyone wants a leader to be proud of for diligent service.

A leader with a vision will build new infrastructures and be named after past heroes of the nation. In Nigeria, established institutions are renamed to score political gains. They rob the renamed institution of its history and, in some cases, established goodwill. The renamed institutions also lose immediate recognition in the country and internationally. This echoes the culture of unintended destruction that is endemic with the leaders.

CONSULAR OFFICE

The Nigerian consular office is the face of Nigeria in another country. It has the function of looking after the interest and welfare of Nigerians in that country. It is the shop window to sell Nigeria to other countries in the world. A place to display patriotism and passion for the country. A place where Nigerians abroad in that country should feel of being at home whenever they visit.

It will not be far-fetched if it is said that you will most likely find Nigerians in almost all countries of the world. Nigeria, as a result, has to offer consular services to its citizens globally. Many embassies or consulates struggle to offer satisfactory services. Poor leadership management and Visionless leaders account for this.

The root course could be how ambassadors are selected for a particular office. It is a failure from the start when the country's representative does not have the nation's interest at heart.

Many consular offices are in remote locations, thus making a visit very difficult and expensive for people. Some offices are unable to meet the high demand for the Nigerian passport. In July 2019, the London office had its property vandalised by a frustrated citizen.

Figure 11.5: Nigerian Embassy Car Vandalised
(Source: Premiumtimes)

This is a failure to generate revenue for the country from people that can afford and are willing to pay for good service. The Nigerian Immigration Service (NIS) has virtually admitted the failure of its policy to allow Nigerians to travel into the country with expired passports.

The head of NIS should have done a clear-out of inept officers. This did not happen because the management team had no clue what good service was. Its members are probably not qualified or experienced enough to hold the positions they have been rewarded with.

A mediocre head cannot command the respect of its team or stakeholders. They all know their shortcomings in their abilities and skills to do the jobs. The mediocrity is allowed to continue throughout the legal term. Every inefficiency and underperformance is allowed to prevail. Infrastructures are, however, being run down, resulting in suffering by the people.

The Nigerian consular offices around the world should be providing intelligent information on how to maximise resources in Nigeria, having had first experiences in other nations. The management of Nigerian resources is not currently the best; this is why knowledgeable representatives should be representing Nigeria abroad. They will use their expertise to achieve collaborations between Nigeria and their hosting nations.

TOURISM

Tourism enriches a nation in so many ways. It creates employment which improves the well-being of the people. The primary factor for tourism anywhere is the safety of people in that society. People are naturally inclined to explore places other than their locality. Travellers and tourists make short and very long journeys in the course of their explorations. There is always an element of insecurity everywhere in the world. However, many places are declared safe to visit.

The consular offices of a country such as Nigeria work with tourism boards to have up-to-date information about different countries. This is to enable them to issue guidelines for tourists.

They provide tourist guides which will include why you must pay a visit to their country, the precautions to take, where to avoid, and things to do and not to do.

A leisure visit primarily takes a break from work to relax by doing thrilling things that stimulate the brain differently. It is the tourist's time to be spent as desired. The holiday is budgeted for, thus removing financial pressure while on holiday. The benefactor is the hosting society, where a holidaymaker has decided to go. This is why every country encourages and supports tourism. Some countries ensure that their citizens are nice and helpful to tourists.

Nigeria happens to be blessed with many features that are attractive to tourists. It can quickly be mentioned here that some tourists just want to go to the capital cities of every country in the world, while for some, it is just to see the major rivers of the world. Not surprisingly, some travel to different places for the food. One popular reason for a place to be a tourist destination is sandy beaches.

Are there sandy beaches in Nigeria? Definitely, from Badagry all the way to Port Harcourt. A lot of untapped wealth exists here in Nigeria. Nigerian beaches are naturally clean and very warm, allowing all-day, all-year fun. The favourable weather conditions in the country should put Nigeria at the top of tourists destinations. Nigeria has, however, not experienced a tourist explosion, mainly due to insecurity.

Nigeria has mountains for climbers, forests for walkers and explorers, and great hotels for people to relax. Nigeria has loads of universities for touring and exchange students who like to embark on exploring different societies. Young men and women take time out of work and studies to tour the world. There are established international routes that these youngsters follow. Their hosts expect them and make them feel welcome during their stay. Nigeria will make its way into the route when safety is no longer an issue.

Nigerian leaders, in the country's interest, should continue the fight against insecurity. Individual Nigerians have the role of positively promoting the country and welcoming all its societies.

THE NATIONAL YOUTH SERVICE CORPS (NYSC)

Every Nigerian graduate must undergo a one-year national service. They are commonly called youth corper or simply "corper" in the year of service. Failure to do national service excludes one from government jobs. A finance minister once lost the job for not being able to confirm doing the service.

It is aimed at giving back to the country, so these graduates are posted to different parts of the country. It was something of pride to do when it started and for the first few years. Like so many things degenerating in Nigeria, including increased insecurity, some areas have become places corpers do all they do to avoid being posted to. Those who get the postings change them to more desirable locations. Attacks on corpers should be taken seriously by all concerned. Everyone in the society should do all they can to ensure their safety.

Corpers were respected members of society, mentors to the younger generations or those yet to undergo a degree programme. They integrate well into their societies, and many end up getting permanent roles where they serve. Their parents and friends pay them visits at their locations, thereby promoting local tourism. They open all corners of the country to people outside the area and the world at large.

Corpers are the wealth of the nation that should be treasured and looked after very well. They are the future entrepreneurs, the chief executives, and the bloodstream of the nation. It is suggested that each corper should be encouraged to take a life insurance cover during their service year.

Questions:

1. Why do corpers include location as important in where they would like to carry out their service year?

2. Design a route that young tourists like school leavers can take to go around Nigeria, considering their vulnerabilities.

3. How can the Nigerian government bring an end to insurgents resurging?

4. Explain why there are continuous cries of separation by some people in Nigeria?

5. What are the functions of the Nigerian consular offices abroad?

6. How can local and international tourism be improved in Nigeria?

7. Why would non-Nigerians want to visit Nigeria for leisure activities?

8. What does it mean to be patriotic?

9. Which Nigerian president can be described as being patriotic and why?

10. Should Nigeria be divided as being demanded by some communities?

CHAPTER

12

GOING FORWARD

The issues highlighted in the pages of this book show the abundance of opportunities available in Nigeria. Many businesses can be set up to counter the waste from wealth burning. It will take time for efficient mass transportation to be established in Nigeria, just as it will take time to upgrade the road networks in the country. Every effort and progress made in one area should be acknowledged, celebrated, and preserved. It should be well maintained and upgraded to contemporary standards as much as possible.

No leader in Nigeria should deter or stop any form of good development in any part of Nigeria because any such positive development is in the best interest of the whole country. It is time to see the country as one and the people as Nigerians rather than individual attributes. Anyone who has naturalised as a Nigerian is a Nigerian, where they originated becomes less significant. This is what makes a nation great. Any leader or individual that sees development in any part of the country as a threat to another part of Nigeria is not fit for any office in the country.

The government and all concerned in the quest for separation from Nigeria should learn to work together peacefully. People agitate for separation because Nigeria and its resources are not well managed in the interest of all Nigerians. The government must admit its failures and take steps to rectify them.

A good government flourishes with good opposition; everyone is at their best to outperform each other, which is to the benefit of the nation. The opposition highlights what is not working or what should be done while the government counters it. A good government does not please everyone all the time but should do what is thought best for the nation all the time.

Imprisonment of people with a different view only creates new oppositions, which will continue until the reason for crying out is addressed. The case of Nelson Mandela should be considered by Nigerian leaders. The potential of freedom fighters and their energies should be explored and used in the interest of the nation. Selfish interest should be in the way of building a better Nigeria.

Leaders of tomorrow should have the right mindset from an early age and not be exposed to corrupt practices. There is a need to encourage collective ownership of the country and hence, collective responsibility for its continual development. Every citizen must be aware that their action and inaction impact the nation. Nigeria will one day have electricity running 24 hours continuously with no interruptions other than because of planned maintenance or natural emergency.

There is a need for all Nigerians to change how they see each other. First and foremost, appreciate one another and do not think you are better or worthier than another Nigerian. It is also important to see each other as Nigerians rather than with tribal and regional connotations. By so doing, everyone is as worthy as the other person.

Every profession should be recognised and cared for simply because each is part of the overall jigsaw called Nigeria. The nation will be healthier with a society where everyone has a sense of ownership and belonging.

Nigerians need to become more relaxed and trust each other to overcome the issue of mistrust. This can be achieved by caring, being nice to fellow Nigerians, and treating everyone respectfully. As stated above, the key is to see every Nigerian as an individual accepting you are not more than the other individual. Everyone is just another Nigerian.

The disgraceful act of Nigerian soldiers fighting or beating Nigerian police officers up and destroying their properties stemming from the notion of superiority should end. They should use their maturity to deal with heated situations calmly. There should be no tension between any of the armed forces and other bodies acting to serve Nigerians. Nigerians who believe they are born to rule should be humble in using their power. They should be prepared to identify the history of failure and change direction in the interest of Nigeria.

This is a failure from the top in that what is expected and accepted behaviour from uniformed officers has not been well communicated. The need for all of the armed forces to work together for all Nigerians must be understood by everyone. This is why the power and authority attached to each post should be earned on merit.

The armed forces have lost able officers through early retirement because of accelerated promotions or fast-tracking of some officers. Again, the practice of not promoting by merit cripples the armed forces. The subordinates only respect the post and not the post holder; they obey instructions only due to the power given to them.

The "na oga pikin" syndrome that has become accepted should be challenged to stop having less competent people in key positions in the Nigerian government. The entrepreneur that plans for a family member to take over the running of their business organisation in the future ensures the person is given sound educational training, coaching, and tests. That person understands the organisation's vision, takes ownership, and appreciates what is at stake. The price of failure is known, so all efforts are directed into the interests of the organisation so it can continue successfully as a going concern. It is not uncommon for the family member not to be up to the task, so the board appoints someone who leads the organisation now and beyond. The board appreciates appointing the incompetent family member because *na oga pikin* will kill the business.

Nigeria's government shoots itself twice, appoints less competent, and retires competent ones. The competent officers lost in the services due to early retirement must continue to be maintained by the government that retired them in the first instance and future governments until they die. A big waste of talent and skills for the nation. The nation's overall interests were not allowed to overrule when decisions were made.

Nigerians will care less about who the president is as long as the citizens are cared for and well looked after. Those who aspire to be leaders must have vision(s) of the transformations they dream for the country. A good leader wins and has the support of the nation's citizens. Other than for legal provisions, the people desire that such government continue for as long as possible.

Good government is credited to the ruling party. Hence, the same party can be in government for many years as long as the people feel they are doing well and the opposition party is unable to show otherwise. The cycle is only broken by complacency by the ruling party. The people easily vote for a new party, not the leader of the failing party.

Separationists will be kept quiet if the government is good, fair, just, and seen to have the interest of the nation at heart. Agitators only rise up when pushed to the wall. The misuse or mismanagement of NNPC's resources is an example of how some people have been forced to cry out for a just society in Nigeria. Many lives have been lost because of this. Many properties, man-hours, and resources have equally been lost, and still, more will be lost for many years until the government is seen to be just.

The president is just another father or mother, uncle or aunty, brother or sister, just like the chef, professor, or tailor in their families. It is a transient post that should be well used to drive the nation as one forward.

Nigerians must stop killing fellow Nigerians because of different political views and affiliations. The people must appreciate with tolerance the value of different opinions and engage in enlightening discussions. Having and being allowed to express different points of view leads to a better understanding of the status quo or innovative practices.

Nigerians must be willing to do everything at the highest possible quality and expect the same high standard from fellow citizens. Give the best, expect the best ask for the best, and decry substandard practices in all areas of society. A society that enthuses a caring attitude will attract people from all over the world.

Nigeria is blessed with everything that people travel for, such as forests, seas with nice sandy beaches, sunshine with relatively high temperatures all year round, and entertainers, to name a few.

Every Nigerian has the potential to be a leader. Artificial barriers should be identified and mitigated to ensure that the nation maximises the potential of its people. By so doing, Nigerians will help themselves out of the unnecessary suffering they are facing to live with from one generation to another.

NIGERIANS MUST CARE FOR NIGERIANS

What do Nigerians care about and care for? What do Nigerians care to do very well? Is it constructing good roads, roads that are designed for all weather and that can withstand extreme loads? Is it the provision of good medical facilities for all leading to good care for all Nigerians and no need for the rich to go abroad for treatment? Is it by caring for fellow Nigerians that there is trust and belief in one another?

Nigerians selfishly or wickedly deprive other Nigerians of goods and services. It is Nigerians that now need to serve fellow Nigerians selflessly and act in the interest of Nigerians.

Caring reveals the value in and of what is being cared for. Valuable things are cared for and looked after by responsible people, which every Nigerian should be. Valuable things are protected from destruction and theft or anything that can lead to deterioration in their value. Nigerians must value one another.

It is better to give than to receive. The law of nature states that for every action, there is an equal but opposite reaction. This means that you get back what you have given one way or the other. The more you give, the more you receive.

It must be highlighted and appreciated that everyone has something to give to care for people. It is not always about money or physical possession that you have to relinquish. The perception of a loss or decrease in what is owned can inhibit the act of giving. It creates the need to first increase what is owned before giving.

Unfortunately, this is where greed creeps in because man's insatiable want has been proven by great economists.

The thought should rather be what can be given to assist in the neighbor's situation. The positive approach will open the options of what is available to be given out. A choice is then made cheerfully.

The receiver, too, must be humble in accepting the offer. No offer should be rejected as being too small; it is a contribution to the full need. Appreciation should always be shown by the receiver to the giver.

"Time is money" is commonly used in the business world. Time is thus very valuable and should be used carefully by all, not just business owners. Valuing one's time enables one to value the other person's time, leading to mutual benefits for all.

Caring is all about looking out for the well-being of other Nigerians. Looking out to make things better for the other Nigerians. Such a caring act delivers a society where most people benefit from the care they offer. Every society thrives on trust and honesty everywhere around the world.

To care for one another includes caring for the physical environment too. It was painful watching Nigerians taking time to sweep their homes and shops clean and pack the rubbish only to take a few steps and throw the trash in gutters.

Figure 12.1: Drain Blocked by Nigerians
(Source: Michael April 2023)

Figure 12.1 above shows a Nigerian who has no care for the physical environment. The sand for the work being done is seen covering the gutter. Nigerians should decry the practice of littering and blocking the facilities.

Questions:

1. Why should Nigerians be more caring and compassionate towards fellow Nigerians?

2. What has caring got to do with an insurgency in Nigeria?

3. What should the Nigerian government do to demonstrate its care for its citizens?

4. Can you trust your neighbour? If not, why?

5. Why should your neighbour trust you?

GLOSSARY

Central Bank of Nigeria, CBN

Controller General, CG

Federal Road Safety Corps, FRSC

Independent National Electoral Commission, INEC

National Drug Law Enforcement Agency, NDLEA

National Electric Power Authority, NEPA

National Intelligence Agency, NIA

Nigerian Ports Authority, NPA

Nigeria Security and Civil Defence Corps, NSCDC

Nigerian National Petroleum Corporation, NNPC

Social media include WhatsApp postings, YouTube

State Security Service, SSS

REFERENCES

https://mo.ibrahim.foundation/news/2018/brain-drain-bane-africas-potential

https://www.worldatlas.com/maps/nigeria

https://www.nairaland.com/2453728/map-ethnic-groups-nigeria-it

https://www.westernpest.com/wp-content/uploads/mosquito-side-view.jpg

www.Solakuti.com

www.theeagleonline.com

ABOUT THE AUTHOR

Micheal Olumuyiwa Famokunwa, the author of this book, is very passionate about Nigeria maximising the readily available resources in the country.

Micheal graduated in Chemical Engineering from Obafemi Awolowo University, Ile-Ife. He spent his national service year at NNPC Petrochemicals, Kaduna. He then moved to the United Kingdom, where he did his master's degree at the University of Westminster in Information Management and Finance.

Michael's hobbies include travelling, driving, farming, and caring for people.

L - #0108 - 270723 - C0 - 210/148/10 - PB - DID3642056